MARTIN LECKEBUSCH
ECHOES OF ETERNITY
125 VIBRANT NEW HYMNS

kevin mayhew

kevin
mayhew

First published in Great Britain in 2018 by Kevin Mayhew Ltd
Buxhall, Stowmarket, Suffolk IP14 3BW
Tel: +44 (0) 1449 737978 Fax: +44 (0) 1449 737834
E-mail: info@kevinmayhew.com

www.kevinmayhew.com

9 8 7 6 5 4 3 2 1 0

ISBN 978 1 84867 965 8
Catalogue No. 1501588

Cover design by Rob Mortonson
© Image used under licence from Shutterstock Inc.
Typeset by Angela Selfe

Printed and bound in Great Britain

Contents

About the author

Martin Leckebusch was born in Leicester in 1962 and educated at Oriel College, Oxford (MA, Mathematics) and Brunel University (MSc, Numerical Analysis). Since graduating he has worked in IT. He and his wife, Jane, have four daughters; their second child, a son, died in 1995. The family live in Gloucester and belong to a Baptist church, but have also been involved in Anglican, Methodist and Pentecostal congregations over the years. In July 2017 he was elected Executive Vice President of the Hymn Society of Great Britain and Ireland. Apart from hymnody, Martin's interests include jazz, crosswords, reading and good curry.

Since 1987 he has written over 500 hymn texts: in addition to this volume see *More than Words* (2000); *Songs of God's People* Volumes 1 (2001) and 2 (2002); *The Psalms: 150 metrical psalms for singing to well-known hymn tunes* (2006); and *Never Let the Songs End* (2010). Many of Martin's texts can also be found on Hymnquest and in a wide range of other collections. Besides writing hymns, he is the author of *New Parables for Today's World* (2008), a collection of contemporary parables with theological reflections; *Let Deserts Bloom: Daily Devotions for Lent* (2011); and *The Call to Partnership* (2016), a series of twelve Biblical character studies. All these volumes are published by Kevin Mayhew.

Martin is keen to see the church equipped for Christian living in the twenty-first century world, and believes that well-crafted and wisely-used contemporary hymns and songs have a vital role to play in that process.

Introduction

A couple of weeks ago I reached an anniversary which was surprising and (for me, at least) significant: thirty years since the Saturday morning when I drafted my first hymn text, subsequently revised and eventually published as 'My Lord, you have examined me'.[1] Thirty years is more than half my life, and it feels like a long time to have been writing hymns; longer than I have lived in any one town, attended any one church or worked for any one employer. In fact, apart from my Christian faith, my years working in IT and my marriage, very little has been with me for longer.

Inevitably, much has changed for me in three decades. Those years have seen the predictable phases of life: raising a family and seeing the children start to move beyond education and into their own adult lives; the ageing and loss of parents; and changes of job, location and home. There have been plenty of delights along the way, but also a share of life's harder challenges: our family, like most, has faced unemployment, health problems, bereavements, and so on. Yet I remain conscious, and thankful, that I have lived through peaceful times in a prosperous country – and mindful that those are things only a minority of the human race consistently enjoy.

I am also aware, though, that there have been other forces at work, for those three decades have seen many changes in the world at large. One obvious turning point in how Western society perceives itself has to be the events of 11 September 2001, which will long stand in history as a significant date. Other events have also made their mark on human society: tragedies such as the death of Diana, Princess of Wales in 1997 and the loss of a quarter of a million lives in the Indian Ocean tsunami of 26 December 2004 have both entered the collective consciousness in the sense that many people remember when and where they first heard the news of those things. Add to that the political upheavals, economic crises, technological advances and environmental disruptions of the past three decades, and life on earth feels somewhat shaken, even in the comfortable West and during a period of relative stability and peace.

For the Church, too, these have been momentous years. In the UK, for example, these decades have broadly coincided with the era which first saw the ordination of women as priests in the Anglican Church; in the West as a whole, Christian adherence has continued a decline which some see as irreversible, while in other parts of the world church growth continues vigorously; and even in the small, safe world of mainstream British denominations, the practice of worship has continued its trend

---

1. 98 in *More than Words: The hymns of Martin E Leckebusch* (2000) and 139 in *The Psalms: 150 metrical Psalms for singing to well-known hymn tunes* (2006), both published by Kevin Mayhew.

away from hymns and entirely oral teaching to more varied expressions of faith, as newer songs, visual presentations and multi-sensory experiences feature more widely than before. There is much here both to challenge and to encourage Western Christians, including hymn writers!

I am aware that many of these events of my lifetime, whether personal or from the wider flow of history, have played a part in shaping who I am, and therefore have also affected my writing; but they have not defined me, for I remain convinced that the core of who I am is a person 'in Christ' as Paul often puts it in his letters,[2] and it is my faith in Christ Jesus which I want to be central to what I write, as to everything I do. Accordingly, while there are hymns in this collection which were directly influenced by the news,[3] I do not generally write in reaction to the headlines. I aim, instead, to produce texts shaped primarily by biblical faith, and to allow the Scriptures to remain a key inspiration for my writing.

Yet neither current affairs nor Scripture is the only factor which encourages me to put pen to paper. The wonder of creation, sermons I have either heard or preached, books I have read, and even chance comments from friends have set in motion trains of thought which ultimately became new texts. One item in this collection, for example, was suggested by the use of the word 'but' in the resurrection accounts[4] while another was inspired by a dream about hymn writing.[5] Several came from quotations[6] or from old prayers or other rites.[7] A few items have been requested, whether for a particular service[8] or as part of a search for hymns on specific themes.[9] One[10] was commissioned for a tune-writing competition, as the text for which entrants were invited to submit new music, while another[11] was itself a runner-up in a text writing competition. Sometimes a piece of music has provided the impetus,[12] though it is more usual for me to start from a theological idea or a verbal phrase than from a tune – I remain a non-musician and in spite of my best efforts at a piano I

---

2. For example, Romans 8:1; 1 Corinthians 1:2; 2 Corinthians 5:17; Ephesians 1:3, 2:10, 4:32.

3. 46, 58 and 121 are key examples.

4. 91

5. I'd rather not say which one!

6. 9, 'Genuine, lasting joy comes from a right relationship with God, with one's neighbours, with oneself and with the earth.' Ronald Sider, from an article in *Tear Times*, 1996; 35, from a mission statement at St Cuthbert's, Wells; 55, from a quotation attributed to Gandhi, cited in *The Soul of Politics*, Jim Wallis (Fount, 1994), pp xi-xii; 64, William Temple, quoted in *Christianity Close to Life*, Rita Snowdon (Fount, 1978), p112; 84, in part from the well-known words of Abraham Kuyper, 'There is not a square inch in the whole domain of our human existence over which Christ, who is Sovereign over all, does not cry: "Mine!"'; 98, 'Follow the light that you have. Pray for more light.' (Iona Community).

7. 13, a prayer variously attributed to both Francis Drake and Walter Raleigh; 18, a prayer from the Community of Aidan and Hilda, in Michael Mitton, *Restoring the Woven Cord* (BRF, 1995, 2010), p135; 19, Vidi Aquam; 20, a Celtic prayer about daily work; 78, the Asperges rite; 105, St Brendan's prayer.

8. 77

9. 34, 45, 48, 75, 97, 117

10. 2

11. 17

12. 119, requested by Kevin Mayhew (but not completed in time for the publication he had in mind).

can usually make the music of W. H. Monk sound like that of Thelonius Monk. In one case, the challenge was the poetic style known as a villanelle.[13]

Whatever its origins, though, a hymn remains a curious artefact. Its text is usually poetic in form, but it is not a poem, being designed for corporate use rather than private reflection or solo recitation; and this distinction places constraints on both its content and its structure. Nor is a hymn primarily a musical item, though a tune is integral to any hymn. Moreover, a hymn tune is designed to be sung by a congregation, rather than being either instrumental or a solo piece, which restricts its range and musical complexity. The text itself is not necessarily a prayer, a doctrinal statement or an instruction, though it can contain all those and more. It must tread several fine lines: between objective and subjective; theology and practice; affirmation and aspiration; personal expression and corporate confession; and emotion, reason and faith. It should be consistent with the Bible and Christian tradition while being open to truth in a changing world. It should be relevant to the lives of those who sing it while never losing sight of the broader story of creation, salvation and re-creation. It should, where possible, speak the language and harness the idioms (whether linguistic or musical) of its intended singers, yet without being enslaved to the prevailing assumptions, values or customs of contemporary culture. Ideally, it should be fresh in its use of both vocabulary and metaphor without being trite or demeaning in its expression. It may be prophetic in content, but it should not be speculative in its message. Its form may appear artificially rigid, with the acceptance of a certain regular pattern of syllable counts, stresses, and rhymes; and its tone and vocabulary should be appropriate for public use. Yet adherence to those very constraints may make it aesthetically satisfying and more likely to lodge in the minds and memories of those who use it. It must be long enough to be worth singing and to contribute to an act of worship, but short enough to fulfil its purpose without dominating a service. Had I realised all of this thirty years ago, I may not have been so eager to embark on the writing of hymn texts.

Yet I did start; and I continue to write, primarily in a traditional style and with established metres in mind. However, as noted earlier, the church in Britain continues to embrace songs and increasingly a genre known as 'modern hymns' – an emerging hybrid style which borrows from both 'hymn' and 'song' and perpetuates the healthy blurring of the boundary between the two. With this in mind, I have been more willing in recent years to adopt a slightly more colloquial style and vocabulary, and this is evident in a few of my newer texts.

This collection contains 125 hymn texts, most of which have seen only limited circulation before now. Almost exactly a hundred of them have been written since 2010, when my last collection[14] was published; among the others there are a couple of very early texts first drafted in 1988, and two more from 1999. In case any readers feel inclined to try to work out which are the oldest texts, I should point out that some of this older material has been extensively revised through the years.

The pattern of indexing in this volume is similar to that in my earlier collections.[15] Selected sources for the suggested tunes are listed. The Church Year and Subject indexes are designed to group texts which have broad similarities of subject matter and applicability; the Thematic index highlights the key words and topics dealt with (or, in some cases, alluded to) in each hymn. The Scriptural index gives some idea of the biblical passages which underpin the writing, whether or not those verses were the direct spur to write the text in question.

---

14. *Never Let the Songs End* (Kevin Mayhew, 2010).
15. *More than Words; The Psalms; Never Let the Songs End.*

Acknowledgements

As ever, I gladly record my numerous debts in hymnody. First and foremost, I am grateful to God for his grace, and specifically for the grace which has been a gift of text writing over the years; may what is written in this book honour him above all.

Secondly, there are various authors whose work has inspired me: Richard E. Bauckham,[16] Carol M. Bechtel,[17] Walter Brueggemann,[18] Olive Fleming Drane,[19] Mark Greene,[20] Gerard Kelly,[21] Derek Kidner,[22] Michael Mitton,[23] Dennis T. Olson,[24] David Prior,[25] W. H. Vanstone,[26] Tom Wright,[27] Philip Yancey[28] and William Paul Young.[29] While thinking of printed books, of course, I remain grateful to Kevin Mayhew, who has published so much of my writing, and to his team.

Next I must mention various individuals who have prompted the creation of new texts, sometimes deliberately and sometimes unwittingly, including: David M. Bailey of Richmond, VA, USA; Kenneth Bowden; Bishop Graham Cray; Martin and Ruth Harrison; Revd Garry Ketchen; Muyiwa Olarewaju; Fr David Patterson of Adelaide, Australia; and Noel Robinson.[30] A number of texts have their origins in the life and worship of Kendal Road Baptist Church, Gloucester, to which I have belonged for over fifteen years.[31] I am also grateful to musicians who have crafted new tunes for my words; texts in this collection have already sparked new music from John Barnard, Paul Drinkwater and Mike Haines.[32] If any musicians can find fresh inspiration in this collection, further new tunes will be welcome, especially for the small

16. 37, from *Jesus and the Eyewitnesses: The Gospels as Eyewitness Testimony* (William B. Eerdmans, 2006).
17. 31, from 'Knowing our Limits: Job's Wisdom on Worship' in *Touching the Altar: The Old Testament for Christian Worship*, ed. Carol M. Bechtel (William B. Eerdmans, 2008).
18. 21, from *Deep Memory, Exuberant Hope* (Fortress Press, 2000), p122.
19. 88, inspired by *Clowns, Storytellers, Disciples* (BRF, 2002).
20. 56, inspired by *The Great Divide* (LICC, 2010).
21. 101, from comments about emphases for the 21st century church in *Get a Grip on the Future Without Losing Your Hold on the Past* (Monarch, 1999).
22. 106; Kidner's exposition of Psalm 61 in *Psalms 1-72: An Introduction and Commentary on Books I and II of the Psalms* (IVP, 1973) highlights the increasingly personal language used through the psalm.
23. 123 was inspired by Mitton, *Restoring the Woven Cord*, chapter 3.
24. 86, from 'Sacred Time: The Sabbath and Christian Worship' in Bechtel (ed), *Touching the Altar*.
25. *The Message of 1 Corinthians: Life in the Local Church* (IVP, 1985), p166, lists 'protection, guidance, sustenance, forgiveness' as reasons for gratitude – see 120.
26. 59, from *The Stature of Waiting* (Darton, Longman and Todd, 1982).
27. 96 draws heavily from *How God Became King* (SPCK, 2012), especially pp151-153.
28. 82, based on the thesis of *What's So Amazing About Grace?* (Zondervan, 1997).
29. 17, from comments in *The Shack* (Hodder, 2008).
30. Respectively, numbers 22; 33 and 91; 57; 53; 79; 71; 19 and 78; 109.
31. In this category are 23, 39, 52, 53, 61, 89,116 and 124. Mention should also be made of number 35, first sung at the opening of Kendal Road's new building, to the tune mentioned below by Mike Haines, who is also a member of this congregation.
32. For numbers 6, 77 and 35 respectively; all three tunes are as yet unpublished.

number of texts which are written to metres or with stress patterns for which I have so far found no tunes.[33]

I mentioned earlier in this introduction the thirtieth anniversary of my first hymn text; the weekend that text was written, Jane and I also celebrated our first wedding anniversary. I remain grateful to her for her support and encouragement over the years, and also to our daughters, Rachel, Hannah, Abigail and Sarah – they, too, have all helped shape both me and these texts.

Finally, one of the particular joys of the past three decades has been membership of the Hymn Society of Great Britain and Ireland,[34] which has brought me into contact with numerous other lovers of hymnody. Some have been eminent writers and composers; most are talented and enthusiastic singers; many have been appreciative and encouraging; and their company, especially at annual conferences, has frequently provoked me to further writing.[35] I dedicate this collection to them all, with gratitude.

Hymns – both those from past generations and those by contemporary writers – remain an important element in my own Christian walk, and one of the ways my faith is nurtured and sustained. I hope that readers of this collection will find here insights and words to encourage and strengthen their own faith.

---

33. 5, 52, 58, 76, 84 and 93 would all benefit in this way.
34. For more details, visit https://hymnsocietygbi.org.uk/.
35. See especially 99, written for a 'home made' hymn festival at the Society's 75th anniversary conference in 2011.

Dedication

For my numerous friends in the Hymn Society, with joyful thanks.

We who gather here are grateful for the richness of our past:
thoughtful words, engaging music – we have loved them, held them fast . . .

We who gather here are hopeful for the days that lie ahead:
talents yet to be discovered, tunes unwritten, words unsaid . . .

1.   Garden

1 A man walked through a garden,
   a verdant gift from God:
   a paradise around him,
   whichever path he trod.
   One fruit he was forbidden –
   yet, thinking he knew best,
   in blatant disobedience
   he failed that crucial test:
      the consequence on history
      has lasted ages long,
      for still we reap the harvest
      of Adam's primal wrong.

2 But to another garden
   there came a second Man:
   his goal, to end the conflicts
   his forebear's sin began.
   No heart can know his struggle
   or feel the pain he felt,
   his sweated blood adorning
   the ground on which he knelt;
      his death secured the pardon
      that cancels human wrong –
      his praise shall be forever
      our glad and grateful song.

Genesis 2:15-17; 3:1-19; Matthew 26:36-39; Mark 14:32-36;
Luke 22:39-44; Romans 5:12-17
Subject index: B.4, G.2, I.6
7 6 7 6 Triple
Suggested tune: *Thaxted*

2. Kingdom drawing near

1 A preacher came from Nazareth
with news for all to hear
of prophecies and hopes fulfilled –
God's kingdom drawing near!
He showed them Israel's holy Lord
as Father, shepherd, friend,
and brought a foretaste of a realm
where love would never end.

2 Then some were angry, some afraid,
though others' hearts were stirred;
a few left all to follow him,
by hardships undeterred.
Though suffering and a brutal cross
defined the path he trod,
they knew his living presence still –
their King, their Lord, their God.

3 Today our praises join their songs –
those saints from ages past
who fought the fight, who kept the faith
and won their race at last.
For righteousness and liberty
they stormed the gates of hell;
their cause, the kingdom they proclaimed,
is ours to share as well.

4 So Christ's unfading call remains
the focus of our lives:
our joyful duty, serving him
until that day arrives
when heaven and earth are new again,
and all God's people sing
and every heart and tongue affirms
that Christ is truly King!

Matthew 10:7; 16:18-19, 21, 24, 25; 19:27; Mark 1:15; 3:5; 8:31, 34-35;
Luke 9:2; 10:1, 9; John 1:45; 20:28; Philippians 1:21; 2:10-11;
2 Timothy 4:7; Revelation 21:1
Subject index: B.3, I.3, J.1
8 6 8 6 D (DCM)
Suggested tunes: *Mornington Crescent* (Oliver Tarney); *Kingsfold*

3.   **Travellers' rest**

1   Ahead we see an open door;
    the room inside is warm and bright.
    The welcome you extend includes
    a table spread for our delight.

2   The journey is too much for us
    unless you give us food to eat;
    but here you break the bread of life –
    our nourishment is made complete.

3   Though thirst assails our weary souls,
    at this, your table, wine is poured;
    in drinking from the living vine
    we find both joy and strength restored.

4   Ahead we see an open door;
    beyond it lies the open way –
    we leave the travellers' rest, equipped
    to journey for another day.

1 Kings 19:7; Psalm 23:5; Matthew 26:26-29; Mark 14:12-25;
Luke 22:14-20; John 6:53-57; 15:5, 11; 20:21
Subject index: H.1, I.6
8 8 8 8 (LM)
Suggested tunes: *Melcombe*; *Fulda*

4.   Unknown

1   An unknown household owned a colt, a youngster:
    unbroken, unprepared for any load;
    and yet, despite the surging throng of pilgrims,
    their noisy shouts, the praises they bestowed,
    this donkey meekly bore the gentle Master
    into the city, on a palm-strewn road.

2   A certain woman brought a jar of perfume
    and poured her costly gift on Jesus' head;
    then some of his disciples were indignant –
    'This should be sold to feed the poor instead!'
    But Christ commended her, and her devotion:
    a burial rite, for soon he would be dead.

3   An unnamed man directed two disciples:
    a house, a room where supper could be laid.
    Here they prepared the meal, as Christ instructed,
    though unaware of all that it portrayed:
    this was the night of Passover's fulfilment,
    a final feast, and then he was betrayed.

4   These unknown saints, these unexpected gestures
    were key as Christ embraced his Father's will;
    these deeds stand out from days of mounting conflict,
    when many fashioned schemes to do him ill.
    Such unselfconscious acts of glad obedience –
    these he recalls, and these he treasures still.

Matthew 10:40, 42; 21:1-9; 25:40; 26:6-13, 17-21; Mark 9:41; 11:1-10; 14:3-9, 12-18;
Luke 19:28-36; 22:7-15; John 12:1-8, 12-15
Subject index: B.4, G.2
11 10 11 10 11 10
Suggested tunes: *Thorpe*; *Finlandia*

5. Turn your smile

1 Be gracious to us, Father,
   and turn your smile towards us;
   may you find pleasure, watching
     the way we spend our days;
   through our lives, show our neighbours
   your faithfulness and greatness,
   till many, many people
     are stirred to sing your praise.

2 For you rule all the nations
   and guide the course of history;
   with every ample harvest
     your kindness crowns the year;
   so, Lord, may you be worshipped
   with songs in every language
   as all the peoples gather
     in joy and holy fear.

Psalm 67
Subject index: F.1, H.5, J.2
7 7 7 6 D

6. Christ, you are present!

1 Beyond the faintest distant star
unknown, unseen by human eye,
beyond the blazing comet-tail
that scores an orbit on the sky,
 Christ, you are present!

2 Beneath the deepest ocean floor,
astride the coldest mountain peak,
across the driest desert sand
where human lips will never speak,
 Christ, you are present!

3 And since that unrecorded dawn,
the birth of time, the first new day,
and on until the cosmic dusk
when final starlight fades away,
 Christ, you are present!

4 Within uncharted mysteries,
unmeasured force and quantum spin;
within the hidden origins
where cells divide and lives begin,
 Christ, you are present!

5 In every beat of every heart,
in every vital draught of air,
and even as we meet the pains
that tempt us downward to despair,
 Christ, you are present!

Psalms 73:23; 139:7-13; Proverbs 8:22-31; Romans 8:35-39;
Colossians 1:17; Revelation 1:17
Subject index: B.6, F.5, J.2
8 8 8 8 5
Suggested tune: *Flaunden* (John Barnard)

7.   Bless the One

1   Bless the One who envisaged and fashioned the earth;
bless the One by whose word its foundations were laid;
  bless God, the creator, the One who is Three;
bless the One who keeps watch over all that he made.

2   Bless the One who is grieved when we stray from his care;
bless the One who was willing to die for our race;
  bless God, the all-holy, the Three who are One;
bless the One who persistently calls us to grace.

3   Bless the One who has spoken to teach us the truth;
bless the One who so faithfully showed us the way;
  bless God, the unchanging, the One who is Three;
bless the One who equips us to hear and obey.

4   Bless the One who reminds us of where we belong;
bless the One who has promised to come back again;
  bless God, the eternal, the Three who are One;
bless the One who is Love, and forever will reign!

Genesis 1:1, 2; Psalm 119:138, 142, 152, 160; Ezekiel 18:32; John 1:1-3; 8:46;
10:17, 18; 14:3, 9; 15:26; 16:8; Romans 5:6-8; 8:16; Galatians 5:16-18;
Ephesians 1:13, 14; Colossians 1:15-17; 1 John 4:8
Subject index: D, F.2, I.2
12 12 11 12
Suggested tune: *Stowey*

8.   **Broken notes**

1   Broken tunes from trembling voices –
     is this all that we can bring?
     Dare we lift such tattered fragments
     as an offering to our King?

2   Jarring chords and diverse rhythms,
     words uncertain and unclear –
     can such rough and strident screeching
     count as music fit to hear?

3   Shouts of joy and cries of anguish,
     countless jumbled tunes and keys –
     will the God of peace and order
     find delight in sounds like these?

4   Yet in this discordant music
     other echoes can be found:
     fears and hopes and pains of living
     blending in a richer sound.

5   Broken notes, yet fair reflections
     of the broken lives we live,
     somehow please our broken Saviour
     as the best that we can give.

Psalm 10:17; 1 Peter 5:7
Subject index: F.5, H.3, I.2
8 7 8 7
Suggested tune: *Sussex*

9.   Lasting joy

1   Come, taste the wine of lasting joy,
      in recognising: God is near!
      In faith discern his gracious touch,
      and understand he holds you dear.

2   As he reveals your faults and strengths,
      allow his Spirit full control –
      be sure of this: the Lord intends
      to make you free, mature and whole.

3   So from the friendship Christ bestows
      may your contentment overflow –
      enrich your neighbours' daily lives
      and bring shalom to those you know.

4   Treat all of God's creation well;
      respect this planet where you live;
      come, savour love and peace and hope,
      the joys your Lord delights to give.

Genesis 2:15; Psalm 16:8, 9; Matthew 10:31; Luke 12:6, 7; John 8:32; 15:15, 17;
Romans 5:2-5; Philippians 2:13; Hebrews 13:2, 5
Subject index: F.5, H.6, J.1
8 8 8 8 (LM)
Suggested tune: *Fulda*

Inclusive language variations
verse 1, lines 2-4: and recognise: the Lord is near!
                    In faith discern love's gracious touch
                    and understand God holds you dear;
verse 2, line 1:   as Christ reveals your faults and strengths,

10.   Dare you

1   Dare you follow if he leads you
to the garden on the hill?
Could you share his painful struggle
to accept his Father's will?
    Or would you, like me, have slumbered
    when the sorrow grew so great,
    too exhausted to be prayerful
    till you found it was too late?

2   Dare you stand as his disciple
when the traitor's plans are laid,
when the soldiers come to seize him
and the Teacher is betrayed?
    Or would you, like me, have faltered,
    tasted fear, and taken flight,
    disappearing from the garden
    under cover of the night?

3   Dare you watch as he is questioned
and be counted as his friend?
Dare you listen for the verdict
that declares his life must end?
    Or would you, like me, have blustered,
    kept your distance, held away,
    till the cock-crow signalled failure
    at the breaking of the day?

4   Dare you venture with the women
through the early morning gloom
as they bear the burial spices
and approach the guarded tomb?
    Or would you, like me, have hidden,
    haunted by remorse and fear,
    snared by doubt – until the moment
    Christ, the wounded Lord, drew near?

Matthew 26:36-56, 58, 69-75; 28:1; Mark 14:32-50, 54, 66-72; 16:1, 2;
Luke 22:39-46, 54-62; 24: 1, 2,11, 12, 34; John 18:15-27; 20:1-7, 19, 20
Subject index: B.4, G.3, H.6
8 7 8 7 D
Suggested tunes: *Corvedale*; *Bethany*

11. Deepen our understanding

1   Deepen our understanding of your love;
make our perception vital, sharp and true;
Lord, may our knowledge of your call increase,
enriching our experience of you.

2   May our discernment blossom and mature;
nourish our faith to meet life's every test;
Lord, shape the pattern of our daily lives
with grace and strength to know and choose the best.

3   So may our hearts be pure and free of blame
until the day we stand before your throne;
Lord, may the harvest of our lives be good,
to make your kindness and your greatness known.

Philippians 1:9-11
Subject index: F.5, H.4
10 10 10 10
Suggested tune: *Go Forth and Tell*

12. Send your Spirit

1   Did you not send your Spirit
     to mark us as your own,
     a people in whose conduct
     your character is shown?
        Then fill us once again, Lord,
        and set our hearts on fire
        to follow Christ's example,
        to live as you desire.

2   Did you not send your Spirit
     to let your people live
     within the perfect freedom
     that you alone can give?
        Then teach our hearts to listen,
        to learn your holy way,
        and make us true disciples,
        who eagerly obey.

3   Did you not send your Spirit
     to make your people one,
     in witness, praise and service
     united in your Son?
        Then by your Spirit's prompting
        renew our mutual care,
        till all your church embodies
        the living hope we share.

Ezekiel 36:26, 27; John 13:35; 14:15, 16, 23-26; 16:13; Romans 8:4, 9;
1 Corinthians 12:13; Ephesians 4:3-5; 5:1; 1 John 3:14
Subject index: C, H.6, I.1
7 6 7 6 D
Suggested tune: *Thornbury*

13.   Disturb us

1   Disturb us, Lord, from easy lives
    which cling to some familiar shore;
    and minds content with little dreams
    which dare not venture, seeking more.

2   Disturb us when the course we set
    is shaped by self-conceit or pride,
    those perils which corrupt the soul
    until the flame of faith has died.

3   Disturb us when our hearts are snared
    by goods we long to call our own,
    which blind us to eternal joys
    and dim our vision of your throne.

4   Disturb us with a restlessness
    which draws us onward, far from land,
    where storms and stars and waves reveal
    your sovereign care, your guiding hand.

Matthew 13:22; Mark 4:19; Luke 8:14; Romans 12:3;
Philippians 2:3; Hebrews 11:13-15
Subject index: F.5, G.3, H.6
8 8 8 8 (LM)
Suggested tunes: *Gonfalon Royal*; *Winchester New*

14.   More to offer

1   Does love have more to offer
    beyond this gift so small,
    a scrap of human frailty
    within a cattle stall?
    This child will grow to manhood
    and youthful, mortal loss:
    God's gift will face rejection,
    stripped bare upon a cross.

2   For God has freely offered
    his one and only Son,
    by whose supreme surrender
    our freedom has been won:
    his pain was our rebellion;
    he died to let us live;
    his sufferings are our healing –
    what more has love to give?

3   The sacrifice is offered,
    this death that means so much –
    now we have reaped love's harvest
    and felt love's deepest touch.
    No more has God to offer,
    no more has love to say
    beyond the call to follow
    love's selfless, giving way.

Isaiah 53:2-5; John 3:16; Romans 8:32; Ephesians 5:2;
Philippians 2:6, 7; Hebrews 10:12
Subject index: B.4, G.1, H.6
7 6 7 6 D
Suggested tune: *Wolvercote*

15.   Draw near

1   Draw near to God with confidence and hope,
    for Christ, our great High Priest, has gone before,
    whose willing death releases guilty hearts
    to mercy, guaranteed for evermore.

2   Draw near, assured to know our gentle King
    has felt the weight of every load we bear;
    how light and gracious are our Lord's demands,
    how keen his hearing for our faintest prayer.

3   Draw near for strength when evil powers entice
    or conflict saps the fervour to obey;
    from Christ himself, who knows how weak we feel,
    comes grace to stand our ground and win the day.

4   Draw near in faith, and meet the living Lord:
    discern his body in the broken bread,
    and in the wine his grateful people share
    recall how, once for all, his blood was shed.

5   Draw near with joy – the music in our hearts
    is but an echo of a deeper call:
    the invitation of the risen Christ
    whose loving welcome offers life to all.

Matthew 11:28-30; John 11:25; 15:16; 1 Corinthians 11:26;
Ephesians 6:13; Hebrews 4:15-16; 10:22
Subject index: B.6, H.2, I.6
10 10 10 10
Suggested tunes: *Woodlands; West Ashton*

16.   Drenched in light

1   Drenched in light, a rustic manger
    where a newborn baby lies;
    drenched in light, the fields, the shepherds –
    angel brightness floods the skies:
        here the gracious Star of Morning
        comes to make his home on earth:
        love's eternal beam is focused
        through a single human birth.

2   Drenched in light, a mountain summit
    brightened by a shining face –
    drenched in light, two honoured prophets
    cross the bounds of time and space;
        here the Servant's call to suffering
        once again is voiced aloud;
        here the Father's affirmation
        echoes from a holy cloud.

3   Drenched in light: the subtle splendour
    of a Lord content to die;
    fading light, a scene of torment
    for a victim lifted high;
        by our Saviour's cross of anguish,
        by his rising from the dead,
        by the light of heaven we follow
        where he leads the way ahead.

Isaiah 53:10; Matthew 17:1-5; Mark 2:14; 9:2-8; Luke 2:7-16; 5:27; 9:28-35;
John 1:14, 18, 43; 12:23, 26-33; Revelation 22:16
Subject index: B.2, G.2, H.6
8 7 8 7 D
Suggested tunes: *Hyfrydol*; *Blaenwern*

17.   God unveils the mystery

1   Each hidden corner of this planet earth
is filled with wonders seen by God alone:
landscapes no human eye has ever scanned;
caverns and canyons unexplored, unknown;
and countless unseen creatures of the deep –
all secrets God has chosen still to keep.

2   Lurking within the atom and the cell,
who knows what particles and forces lie?
Where planets orbit undiscovered stars,
who sees what colours light the evening sky?
Only the One who treasures in his hand
this complex cosmos he alone has planned.

3   Even within a single mortal heart,
who sees the worst, or can discern the best?
Who knows what love or cruelty may emerge,
drawn by some fierce and unexpected test?
None but the God who shaped the human mind
can tell what marvels we have yet to find.

4   Humbly, in sheer amazement, let us bow,
gladly adoring one so great, so wise,
stunned to recall how this amazing God
unveils the mystery of love's great surprise:
our God, on whom the universe depends,
has known us each by name, and called us friends.

Job 38, 39; Psalm 19:1, 12; Isaiah 40:26;
Jeremiah 10:12; 17:9; John 15:15; Acts 17:28
Subject index: A.2, F.3, G.1
10 10 10 10 10 10
Suggested tune: *Yorkshire* (Stockport)

Inclusive language variations
verse 2, line 6: this complex cosmos God alone has planned.

18.   The wisdom of your word

1   Father, by your commanding voice
    the seeds of life were stirred;
    now in expectant, holy fear
    I yield my heart again to hear
    the power of your word.

2   Jesus, in you, the word made flesh,
    the call of God is heard;
    as your disciples once drew near
    I come today, and ask to hear
    the guidance of your word.

3   Spirit of God, I honour you,
    the gift my Lord conferred;
    say all that you know I must hear,
    and deep within my heart make clear
    the wisdom of your word.

Genesis 1:11, 12; Luke 8:9; John 1:14;
1 Corinthians 2:10, 11; Hebrews 1:1, 2; 4:12
Subject index: D, E, H.6
8 6 8 8 6
Suggested tune: *Gatescarth*

19.   Flowing water

1   Flowing water, flowing water
    from the temple of the Lord:
    alleluia for the blessings
    from God's presence, freely poured.

2   Not some ancient mystic vision,
    but God's vibrant Word today:
    Christ, who satisfies our thirsting,
    is the true and living way.

3   Alleluia! Christ, who frees us
    from the barren wastes of sin,
    gives his promised Holy Spirit –
    living waters, deep within.

4   Glory! Father, Son and Spirit,
    threefold One whom we adore –
    glory as at the beginning,
    glory now and evermore.

Ezekiel 47:1; John 7:37-39; 14:6; Romans 5:5;
Colossians 1:13; Revelation 4:8
Subject index: D, F.4, H.1
8 7 8 7
Suggested tune: *All for Jesus*

20. Work to do

1 For times when we have work to do
   we thank you, gracious Lord:
   for challenge and for dignity,
   for purpose and reward.

2 Our skills, our time, our energies,
   the things we plan or make –
   may all the duties we perform
   be done for Jesus' sake.

3 To those with whom we share the task
   and those we serve each day,
   may all our labours illustrate
   our humble Master's way.

4 We face the strains of drudgery,
   the lures of compromise:
   for pressure, make your people strong;
   for conflict, make us wise.

5 Though work be hard or hard to find
   we thank you, gracious Lord,
   that you remain our dignity,
   our purpose, our reward.

Genesis 2:15; Ecclesiastes 2:24; 6:16-20; Jeremiah 9:24; Matthew 10:28-30;
Mark 10:43, 44; 1 Corinthians 1:31; 11:1; Philippians 2:7; Colossians 3:17, 23
Subject index: B.3, H.6, J.1
8 6 8 6 (CM)
Suggested tune: *University*

21.   **Release us**

1   From empty shells of worship
    and dry, dishonest prayer,
    from sterile noise that stifles
    the cry for loving care,
    from futile, rigid dogmas
    that quench the Spirit's fire –
    release us from the rituals
    that sap the soul's desire.

2   From slick and easy answers
    that leave the facts behind,
    from esoteric writings
    that titilate the mind,
    from pointless speculations
    of little real concern
    release us to the challenge
    of truth we need to learn.

3   From lust for endless conquests
    and empire-building schemes,
    from arrogant expansion
    and tyrants' hollow dreams,
    from brutal money-markets
    and skewed, dishonest trade –
    release us from the prisons
    our human greed has made.

4   Release us to the wonder
    of open ears and eyes
    that glimpse eternal beauty
    in mystery and surprise;
    release us to the wildness
    no mortal mind can tame:
    God, through your sacred summons
    reveal your holy name.

Psalm 8:3, 4; Proverbs 28:12; Ecclesiastes 5:10; Isaiah 5:8; 55:6-9;
Amos 5:21-23; 8:5, 6; Luke 18:9-14; John 8:31, 32; Romans 1:20;
Philippians 3:19; 1 Timothy 4:7; 2 Timothy 3:7
Subject index: A.3, F.5, J.1
7 6 7 6 D
Suggested tune: *Aurelia*

22.   From the garden to the city

1   From the garden to the city –
    that's the story of our race:
    from those innocent beginnings
    to the perfect healing-space.

2   Since our forebears in the garden
    were enticed to greed and pride,
    we've been vagrants, running, hiding
    from the God we've all defied.

3   But in Christ this God pursued us,
    drew the plans for our release,
    came among us, faced our hatred,
    died to bring us lasting peace.

4   Now we're called to hope and wholeness,
    children of the loving God,
    a community of pilgrims
    on the pathway Jesus trod.

5   Heirs of God's eternal city,
    we are working for the day
    when the kingdom Christ has promised
    drives injustice right away.

6   From the garden to the city –
    that's the journey of our race
    with the God who calls us homeward
    till we see him face to face.

Genesis 2:8, 15, 25; 3:1-10; Psalms 97:2; 139:7, 8, 11, 12;
2 Corinthians 5:19; Ephesians 2:14-18; Philippians 3:12-14, 20;
Hebrews 1:8, 9; 11:10, 13-16; 1 Peter 1:20; 2 Peter 3:13; 1 John 3:2;
Revelation 21:1, 2; 22:1, 2
Subject index: G.2, I.2, J.4
8 7 8 7
Suggested tune: *Shipston*

23. Daily bread

1 From the wealth of your provision,
Lord, we ask for daily bread;
from creation's rich abundance
may our mouths be fed.

2 Keep us faithful, humble, thankful,
mindful of the things you said;
as we trust our loving Father
may our joy be fed.

3 Where we might be cold and selfish,
give us open hearts instead,
eager in pursuit of justice –
may your world be fed!

4 When we gather at your table,
thinking how your blood was shed,
may we recognise your presence –
may our faith be fed.

5 Stir our vision for the future,
for the joyous feast ahead,
for your kingdom's wedding banquet –
may our hopes be fed.

6 So throughout our journey, give us
every day our daily bread;
for the strength to serve your kingdom,
Lord, may we be fed.

Psalm 65:9-11; Isaiah 58:7; Matthew 6:11, 31-33; 10:8; 26:26-28;
Mark 14:22-24; Luke 11:3; 12:29-31; 22:19, 20; Revelation 19:7
Subject index: G.3, H.3, I.6
8 7 8 5
Suggested tune: *St Leonard's* (Gould)

24. Beyond, among, within

1 God beyond us, who can fathom
light-year distance, curving space?
You have scattered through the cosmos
fingerprints for us to trace.

2 God among us, walking, working,
telling stories, sharing bread,
you defined life's joy and purpose
dying, rising from the dead.

3 God within us: vital presence,
holy heartbeat, always near,
speaking wisdom, challenge, comfort –
you know all we need to hear!

4 God beyond, among, within us,
God we cannot comprehend,
hear our love, our joy, our wonder,
great creator, closest friend.

Psalms 8:1; 16:8; 19:1; Isaiah 40:26; 55:9; Matthew 13:34; 14:13-21;
Mark 4:33; 6:30-43; Luke 9:12-17; John 1:14; 6:1-13; 14:15-17, 25-27;
15:15; 16:13; 2 Peter 1:16
Subject index: D, F.5, H.6
8 7 8 7
Suggested tune: *Gott Will's Machen*

25. Your kingdom's reach

1 God, grant to us a sense of place,
   and make us understand
   earth's hills and plains, our streets and homes
   are held in your strong hand,
       until our dreams of empire fade,
       and we resolve instead
       to see your kingdom's reach extend
       down every path we tread.

2 God, grant to us a sense of time
   beyond this age we know,
   to glimpse the vast realities
   of history's broader flow,
       until we value every day
       and harness every year
       as opportunities to bring
       your coming kingdom near.

3 God, grant a sense that we belong
   in one community
   who name your Son as Lord, and seek
   your Spirit's unity,
       until we prize each other's gifts,
       relieve each other's woes,
       and share the servant way of Christ
       by which your kingdom grows.

4 God, grant to us a greater sense
   of all that you require;
   God, may your call pervade our thoughts
   and set our hearts on fire
       until, before your holy will,
       our selfish longings bow –
       so may we seek your kingdom, Lord,
       together, here and now.

Psalm 24:1; Isaiah 46:10; Matthew 6:10; John 13:12-15; Romans 12:3-6;
Galatians 6:2; Ephesians 4:3, 4; 5:15, 16; Philippians 2:3
Subject index: A.2, I.2, J.1
8 6 8 6 D (DCM)
Suggested tune: *Coe Fen*

26. **God of mercy**

1   God of mercy, show us kindness
    more than we dare rightly ask;
    end our selfish dreams and habits;
    take our stubborn wills to task.

2   God of mercy, bruise us gently
    with the touch we fear, yet need;
    only when your hand restrains us
    can our captive hearts be freed.

3   God of mercy, in compassion
    wield again your surgeon's knife;
    make incisions for our healing,
    vital wounds for saving life.

4   God of mercy, cool the fevers
    raging deep in every soul;
    staunch the wounds that sap our vigour;
    make us holy, make us whole.

5   God of mercy, gracious Saviour,
    you have pledged to make us new,
    one with Christ in death and rising –
    we will place our trust in you.

Isaiah 1:5, 6; Hosea 6:1, 2, 5; John 15:1, 2; 2 Corinthians 5:17;
2 Timothy 2:11, 12; Hebrews 12:5-7
Subject index: F.6, G.2, H.1
8 7 8 7
Suggested tune: *All for Jesus*

27.   **Always now**

1   God, outside time yet always present,
    God, beyond space but always near,
    yours is the wisdom that can guide us;
    yours is the voice we need to hear.

2   You see the end from the beginning;
    you saw our present from our past;
    you know our future in our present –
    you are eternal, First and Last.

3   We, who are time-bound, finite creatures,
    often confused, and prone to stray,
    ask you for insight, faith and courage:
    help us to serve you day by day.

4   Stirred by the promptings of your Spirit,
    may we discern our Saviour's word;
    may we, in honest, swift obedience,
    answer the call that we have heard.

5   God, always now and always near us,
    lead us, and help us understand
    your great adventure, and our purpose –
    our role in all that you have planned.

Proverbs 3:6; Isaiah 57:15; Ephesians 1:18, 19; 3:4, 5; 5:10; Philippians 1:9, 10;
Hebrews 3:15; 13:5; James 1:5; 2 Peter 1:5-7; Revelation 22:13
Subject index: A.2, F.5, H.6
9 8 9 8
Suggested tune: *Spiritus Vitae*

28.   Call to liberty

1   God who freed a captive people
    from a brutal tyrant's hold,
    God whose gift of new beginnings
    far outclasses plundered gold,
        may our hearts be truly free
        through your call to liberty.

2   God who sensed a nation's terror
    through a cataclysmic night,
    God of reassuring presence –
    guiding cloud, and beacon bright –
        through confusion, doubt or fear,
        help us trust that you are near.

3   God who knew your people's hunger
    when they grumbled to be fed,
    God who graciously provided
    forty years of heaven-sent bread,
        may we see, in every meal,
        your unfailing care made real.

4   God whose words revealed a framework
    for the shaping of their days,
    God whose heart would be reflected
    as they learned and walked your ways,
        may our minds and lives stay true
        to the truth we hear from you.

Exodus 12:31-36; 14:10-14, 19; 16:3, 4, 11-15, 20, 35; Leviticus 11:45;
Matthew 6:25, 26; John 8:31, 32; 13:17; Hebrews 13:5
Subject index: A.4, G.3, I.2
8 7 8 7 7 7
Suggested tunes: *Patrixbourne*; *All Saints*

29.   **Open-handed**

1   God whose open-handed giving
          crowns every day,
     God of sharing, God of plenty,
          what can we say?
     Every meal set out before us,
     homes that you provided for us –
     all are signs that reassure us
          love guides our way.

2   God whose open-hearted welcome
          we freely share,
     God whose holy joy and mercy
          reach everywhere,
     through the many trials behind us
     you have never failed to find us,
     faithful always to remind us
          how much you care.

3   God whose open-ended kindness
          your world displays,
     God whose zest for truth and beauty
          sets hearts ablaze,
     for the wealth of all creation,
     love that touches every nation,
     and the joy that is salvation
          we sing your praise.

Deuteronomy 8:2; Psalm 65:11-13; Acts 2:39; 14:17; 17:25;
Romans 5:5; 15:13; James 1:5; 1 Peter 1:8, 9
Subject index: A.2, F.4, G.2
8 4 8 4 8 8 8 4
Suggested tune: *Worthy the Lamb*

30.   Holy mystery

1   God whose ways surpass the visions
        seen by humankind,
    God whose thoughts defy the probing
        of the keenest mind,
    hear our cry for understanding
        for the troubled times we find.

2   Though we shout or weep in turmoil,
        still we find you near –
    when we come with honest questions,
        thank you that you hear;
    give us courage, give us patience
        till you make your answers clear.

3   Are you not the God of history,
        still at work today?
    In the midst of pain or peril,
        can we know your way?
    When the facts seem harsh or complex,
        does your mercy still hold sway?

4   God, we cannot sound your motives
        from our finite view,
    nor demand your explanation
        for the things you do;
    God of justice, good and faithful,
        help us fully trust in you.

5   Lord, we bow before a wisdom
        far beyond our own:
    God eternal, holy mystery,
        high on heaven's throne,
    through our doubts, our joys, our struggles,
        may we find your love made known.

Job 38:2; Psalm 86:5-7, 15; Ecclesiastes 5:2, 3; Isaiah 55:8, 9; 57:15;
1 Corinthians; 1:9; James 2:13
Subject index: A.3, F.5, J.2
8 5 8 5 8 7
Suggested tune: *Angel Voices*

31.   **Wild and free**

1   God, wild and free, wondrous and fearsome,
    you are a whirlwind no force can restrain;
    you are a fire, fierce and consuming;
    you are a river no dam would contain.
        Awed by your splendour we humbly bow;
        freely we offer you our worship.

2   God, wise and pure, holy and timeless,
    you are the author of mysteries untold;
    yours is the hand fashioning history;
    you are the cauldron where lives become gold.
        Drawn by your purpose we humbly bow;
        freely we offer you our worship.

3   God, strange and strong, trusted tormentor,
    you are the surgeon whose scalpel we fear;
    you are the sleuth probing our darkness;
    you are the lover who beckons us near.
        Held in your keeping we humbly bow;
        freely we offer you our worship.

Job 12:13; Psalm 93:2; Isaiah 6:3; 26:4; 28:2; 66:15;
Daniel 2:20-22; 4:3; Malachi 3:3; Hebrews 12:29
Subject index: A.3, F.2, H.4
9 10 9 10 9 9
Suggested tune: *Earth and All Stars*

32. Love among us

1 God's gift to us today is love:
  the love that Jesus Christ has shown,
  that captivates our minds and hearts
  and claims us as his own.
      Lord, hear us – how glad we are
      that this love of yours reaches near and far;
      Lord, thank you for all we feel
      of your gift of love among us.

2 Around us, in so many ways,
  the love of God is still revealed:
  it welcomes, nurtures, soothes and builds,
  till hearts and homes are healed.
      Lord, work through the lives we lead:
      make us each the answer to someone's need.
      Lord, show us what we must do
      with your gift of love among us.

3 We join today with bride and groom
  to celebrate the love they share,
  to watch as they commit themselves
  to lifelong mutual care.
      Lord, answer us now, we pray:
      may your joy and peace fill this wedding day!
      Lord, grant us a lasting sense
      of your gift of love among us.

4 God's call to us today is love:
  to share the kindness Christ made known,
  to give, to listen, care and serve,
  to make his way our own.
      Lord, change us, till all we do
      makes the people round us aware of you;
      Lord, teach us the breadth and depth
      of your gift of love among us.

Omit v3 for a general hymn; include v3 for a wedding hymn
Psalm 103:11; John 13:34, 35; 1 Corinthians 13:7; Ephesians 3:17-19;
1 John 3:1, 16, 23; 4:7, 11, 20, 21
Subject index: F.5, G.1, H.6
8 8 8 6 7 10 7 8
Suggested tune: *Greensleeves*

33. Lord, keep us true

1 Have you not opened our hearts by the truth that you told us?
Did you not promise release from the powers that
controlled us?
Lord, keep us true,
and as your word makes us new
so may your calling uphold us.

2 Make us consistent – our speaking, behaving, believing;
when you uncover our faults, may our hearts be found
grieving.
Lord, keep us true,
faithfully walking with you,
your mercy daily receiving.

3 So keep our faith moving onward, avoiding stagnation –
fire us with hope for a cosmos released from frustration!
Lord, keep us true,
eager to see all you do
as you complete our salvation.

Psalm 51:4, 9, 12; John 8:32, 36; Romans 8:22-25;
1 Corinthians 1:8, 9; Philippians 3:16
Subject index: F.5, H.6, I.2
14 14 4 7 8
Suggested tune: *Lobe den Herren*

34. Hunger that wounds

1   Have you not planted in the human spirit
    a restlessness we cannot satisfy?
    Have you not set eternity within us,
    a taste that haunts us till the day we die?
    Have you not fostered in our lives a hunger
    that wounds our hearts, and makes us question why?

2   The tides of life flow ever back and forward;
    relentless trends and seasons cycle round.
    In happy, healthy times our dreams can flourish;
    in war or pain, our hopes are run aground.
    Through all this change, contentment seems elusive,
    and deep, pervasive joy is rarely found.

3   However far we travel life's adventure,
    however fine or rare the skills we hone,
    however close the friends we trust and cherish,
    however great the wealth we call our own –
    all these together cannot yield fulfilment
    that we were made to find in you alone.

4   Lord, may we hear, within our deepest yearnings,
    your Spirit's whisper, urging us to come
    and find, in walking humbly with our Maker,
    our human purpose and our true shalom –
    so may we recognise the love that formed us,
    that calls our names, and longs to lead us home.

Ecclesiastes 2:10, 11; 3:1-8,11,15; Micah 6:8
Subject index: F.5, G.3, J.2
11 10 11 10 11 10
Suggested tune: *Finlandia*

35.   Sacred space

1   Help us, Lord Jesus, here to weld
the loving bonds of unity,
where open, friendly smiles reveal
a welcoming community,
    till this becomes a sacred space
    where all enjoy your warm embrace.

2   Help us, Lord Jesus, join in praise
for love that makes the heart rejoice,
with worship's fire in every soul
and eager songs from every voice,
    till this becomes a sacred space,
    a house of joy, a thankful place.

3   Help us, Lord Jesus, tune our thoughts
to sense our neighbours' weighty cares;
help us express life's brokenness
in wordless cries, in earnest prayers,
    till this becomes a sacred space
    whose peace reflects your Father's face.

4   Help us, Lord Jesus: stretch our faith
in minds renewed and spirits stirred,
in lives responsive to your call,
the challenge of your vital word,
    till this becomes a sacred space
    for training in the life of grace.

Psalms 133; 134; Luke 17:5; John 13:34; Romans 5:2, 5; 1 Corinthians 14:15;
Galatians 6:10; 1 Timothy 2:1; Hebrews 10:24, 25; James 1:22
Subject index: G.3, H.6, I.3
8 8 8 8 88
Suggested tunes: *New Kendal* (Mike Haines); *Melita*

36.   **Another day**

1   Here is another day:
    now, as the hours unfold,
    what are its joys and pains,
    what will the minutes hold?
        Our gracious Saviour, keep us true
        to spend today in serving you.

2   Some will enjoy success;
    some fear their plans will fail;
    some face the day with strength;
    others are feeling frail;
        come, Holy Spirit, draw us near:
        renew our hope, dispel our fear.

3   Will there be endless toil,
    more than the heart can bear?
    Will there be space to grow,
    time to create or care?
        Our gracious Saviour, keep us true
        to spend today in serving you.

4   Some need to make a choice
    setting their future way;
    some will receive a shock –
    stress that disrupts the day:
        come, Holy Spirit, draw us near:
        renew our hope, dispel our fear.

5   Here is another day –
    show us the way to live,
    how to enjoy and use
    this precious gift you give:
        our gracious Saviour, keep us true
        to spend today in serving you.

Psalm 90:12; Proverbs 27:1; Ecclesiastes 2:22; John 16:33; Romans 12:1, 2;
Galatians 6:9, 10; Ephesians 5:10; Colossians 3:17
Subject index: F.5, H.6, J.1
6 6 6 6 8 8
Suggested tune: *Little Cornard*

37. Glory

1   His splendour far surpasses shining stars and moon and sun –
a light that blazed when even time itself had not begun,
a voice that spoke in power, and so creation's work was done:
  the glory was Christ's own.

2   Through water that he turned to wine on someone's
    wedding day;
through blindness changed to sight, and lifelong darkness
    sent away;
through some he raised to life again, defeating death's decay,
  Christ's splendour has been shown.

3   Then came his hour of glory in the midst of darkest night:
the powers of evil played their hand and strove to quench
    the light;
in willing self-surrender Christ embraced that fiercest fight –
  a cross became his throne!

4   This glory born of suffering is the call his people share:
to heed his Spirit's prompting, and to demonstrate his care.
Through all who follow Christ and through the lasting fruit
    they bear
  God's glory will be known.

John 1:14; 2:1-11; 9:1-11; 11:38-44; 12:27; 13:34; 14:25, 26, 30, 31; 15:8; 16:14; 17:5;
Hebrews 1:3
Subject index: B.1, H.6
14 14 14 6
Suggested tune: *Vision*

38.   Always near

1   Holy Father, may your presence
    guide me all my days,
    moulding every thought and habit,
    every turn of phrase:
    keep me open to the challenge
    brought by your all-seeing gaze.

2   In those all-important moments
    choosing right or wrong,
    may the knowledge you are with me
    keep me true and strong;
    may your Spirit's timely prompting
    make me faithful all day long.

3   Time and tide may rage against me,
    yet your word is clear:
    in my shifting circumstances,
    you are always near!
    Your joy is my lasting comfort;
    your love conquers all my fear.

4   May the sense that you have called me
    shape the path I trace,
    leading me beyond the shadows
    cast by sin's disgrace
    till, at last, I stand before you –
    till I see you face to face.

Exodus 20:20; Psalms 19:12-14; 139:1-4; John 21:18; 1 Corinthians 13:12;
2 Corinthians 5:10; Hebrews 13:5; 1 John 4:14
Subject index: F.5, G.3, H.4
8 5 8 5 8 7
Suggested tune: *Angel Voices*

39. Holy, holy, holy

1   Holy, holy, holy Father,
    wise before the world began,
    flawless love and perfect justice
    meet in your eternal plan.

2   Holy, holy, holy Saviour,
    bearing grief and shame and loss,
    we are rescued, healed and welcomed
    by your anguish, by your cross.

3   Holy, holy, holy Spirit,
    breath of life, unending fire,
    you unleash transforming powers
    far beyond our hearts' desire.

4   God of holy, holy splendour,
    we have heard your pressing call;
    work in power, love and wisdom
    in us each, and in us all.

Psalm 85:10; Isaiah 6:3; 53:4-6; Jeremiah 10:12; John 17:11; Acts 2:2-4;
1 Corinthians 1:30; 2 Corinthians 3:18; Philippians 2:13
Subject index: D, F.2, I.2
8 7 8 7
Suggested tune: *Love Divine*

40.   How can we claim

1   How can we claim to love you, God our Maker,
    if we disdain the brother at our side?
    What kind of love would let us scorn our sister,
    despising one for whom our Saviour died?

2   Can we love you, but fail to help your people
    struggling with burdens few have strength to bear?
    Can we love you, and not see how, around us,
    are some with hardships we refuse to share?

3   If words alone are what we choose to offer,
    if we avoid the costly, helpful deed,
    dare we pretend the God of love is with us
    while we ignore a neighbour's pressing need?

4   Dare love be passive when the call is urgent?
    Dare love stay silent when the cause is just?
    Should love not lead the challenge to oppression
    when joy is crushed, and hopes are ground to dust?

5   Lord, help us see your face in those around us
    whose needs, compelled by love, we strive to meet,
    till, as our strength is spent in willing service,
    we find your love in us is made complete.

Proverbs 3:27, 28; Isaiah 58:9, 10; Matthew 25:31-40; Luke 10:36, 37;
Galatians 6:2; James 2:15, 16; 1 John 3:17, 18; 4:12; 5:20, 21
Subject index: F.6, H.3, I.4
11 10 11 10
Suggested tune: *Intercessor*

41.   Gethsemane

1   How dark it is, this night
    before the darkest day:
    we contemplate this holy place
    with wonder and dismay.

2   Among these olive trees
    kneels Christ, in deep distress:
    the call he hears, the load he bears,
    no language can express.

3   He peers into the cup
    his Father bids him drain –
    and sees a depth of suffering there
    beyond mere mortal pain.

4   His sweat, like drops of blood,
    falls heavy on the ground;
    he yields before the sacred call,
    and new resolve is found.

5   The call remains the same,
    but God has heard his cry:
    he leaves Gethsemane content
    to suffer and to die.

Matthew 26:36-46; Mark 14:32-42; Luke 22:39-46
Subject index: B.4, F.2, I.6
6 6 8 6 (SM)
Suggested tune: *Trentham*

42.   **I will not let you go**

1   How stubbornly the human heart
pursues each hollow aim;
how stridently demanding power,
or pleasure, wealth or fame.
We scorn the summons to obey
God issued long ago;
at times his words seem like a threat:
'I will not let you go.'

2   Then harsh and troubled times expose
our frailty, folly, fear:
our vigour shrivels when we find
despair and danger near;
but on the precipice of life
with emptiness below,
there comes an echo, breathing hope:
'I will not let you go.'

3   For through the years our patient God
fulfils his greater goal:
a faithful people, won by love,
restored, at peace, made whole;
he shows his wisdom, step by step,
until at last we know
the tender love behind those words:
'I will not let you go.'

Deuteronomy 31:6, 8; Jeremiah 17:9; John 10:27-29; Romans 8:28-30;
Philippians 1:6; Hebrews 13:5; 1 Peter 4:12; 1 John 2:16
Subject index: A.4, G.2, H.6
8 6 8 6 D (DCM)
Suggested tune: *Coe Fen*

Inclusive language variations
verse 1, line 7: at times the words seem like a threat:
verse 3, line 2: fulfils a greater goal:
verse 3, line 5: God shows us wisdom, step by step

43.   I came to you, Lord

1   I came to you, Lord, with much to confess –
the guilt of a lifetime's rebellion, no less –
but you were so gracious, forgiving my sin,
enabling a new way of life to begin.

2   I came to you, Lord, too weak for the fight,
too snared by old habits to do what was right –
but you saw my shackles and broke them away
to give me the freedom and strength to obey.

3   I came to you, Lord, so riddled with fear,
appalled at the prospect of death looming near –
but you showed me dying was simply the door
to your perfect presence – my home evermore.

John 8:34, 36; 14:1-3; Romans 6:14-18; Colossians 1:13, 14;
1 Thessalonians 4:17; Hebrews 2:14, 15; 1 John 1:9
Subject index: G.3, H.1, I.2
10 11 11 11
Suggested tune: *Slane*

44.   I offered

1   I offered you an acorn,
    compact and self-contained;
    it shrivelled in the garden
    till none of it remained.
        I offered you an acorn –
        but you have given me
        a sapling with the promise
        to make a towering tree.

2   I offered you a blossom,
    a gentle, fragile flower
    whose beauty and whose fragrance
    might barely last an hour;
        I offered you a blossom
        but you made it complete
        by fruit you formed and nurtured –
        full-grown and ripe and sweet.

3   I offered you my longings:
    to build a holy place,
    to make for you a dwelling,
    a home in time and space;
        I offered you my longings –
        yet these can be fulfilled
        by nothing but the kingdom
        you always planned to build.

4   I offered you my struggles,
    the hardships I had faced,
    the days of sheer frustration,
    of wilderness and waste;
        I offered you my struggles –
        and as you heal my pain
        your character, your kindness
        will show through me again.

        And all I dreamed of giving,
        you knew it long before –
        whatever I have offered,
        my Lord, you give me more.

Psalm 132:2-5,13, 14; Luke 6:38; Galatians 4:19; Ephesians 4:24; James 1:5
Subject index: F.5, H.4
7 6 7 6 D
Suggested tune: *Salley Gardens*

45. **Peace renewed**

1   In the stillness of the morning
    when I wake, and day is new,
    Father, may your promised presence
        draw my thoughts to you.

2   Through the never-ending clamour
    of the most demanding day,
    may your Spirit's inner prompting
        show me Jesus' way.

3   And at times when circumstances
    force me into solitude,
    may I find my heart is nurtured
        and my peace renewed.

4   In the welcome calm of evening,
    through the darkest night-time hour,
    Father, may I rest securely
        in your loving power.

Deuteronomy 3:16; Psalms 3:5, 6; 5:3; Isaiah 30:21; Lamentations 3:25, 26;
Zephaniah 3:17; John 14:26; 16:33; Hebrews 13:5
Subject index: D, F.5, H.6
8 7 8 5
Suggested tune: *St Leonard's* (Gould)

46.   I know

1 In times of stress and grief,
   when terror feeds on fear,
   may your voice answer cries of pain –
      'I know, I see, I hear.'

2 When evil forces wreck
   what peaceful minds have planned,
   may your word comfort troubled hearts –
      'I know, I understand.'

3 When justice is attacked
   and wavers in despair,
   we need your promised strength and peace –
      'I know, I watch, I care.'

4 When even age-old wounds
   still chafe like iron bars,
   your deep compassion reaches out –
      'I know, I feel your scars.'

5 Lord Jesus, take your church
   and in our lives reveal
   the truth that kindles hope and joy –
      'I know, I love, I heal.'

Exodus 15:26; Psalms 23:4; 44:22, 23; 56:4-6, 8; 80:3-5; 82:1-4; 86:7; 116:15; 147:3;
Proverbs 15:3; Isaiah 40:27, 28; 42:3; John 16:33; 1 Peter 5:9
Subject index: F.5, G.2, H.3
6 6 8 6 (SM)
Suggested tune: *Sandys*

47.   I called to you

1   In years gone by, when troubles came upon me,
    when pressure grew till all I felt was fear,
    and when the threads of life itself seemed fragile,
    I called to you, believing you would hear.

2   I called to you amid those swirling waters,
    amid the storms that nearly made me drown,
    although it seemed that you were my tormentor
    who sent the surging waves to press me down.

3   Deep down I sank, beneath a weight of anguish
    to face the threat of unremitting night;
    but you, my Lord, renewed my hope and saved me,
    releasing me from snares whose grip was tight.

4   Can I forget my promises to serve you?
    Dare I ignore your faithfulness to me?
    I will renew my gratitude and worship;
    yours, yours alone, forever I shall be.

Jonah 2
Subject index: F.4, G.3, H.4
11 10 11 10
Suggested tune: *Intercessor*

48.   Master and Mentor

1   Jesus our Teacher,
    Master and Mentor,
    how can we rightly
        answer your call?
    How can our lives be
    shaped to your purpose?
    How can we honour
        you above all?

2   Show us the values
    we must embody;
    show us the vision
        we must pursue;
    take us, and make us
    lifelong disciples –
    we are apprenticed,
        learning from you.

3   Your life has shown us
    life as it should be;
    your word is counsel
        apt for our need;
    your Spirit's prompting
    stirs us to action,
    serving wherever
        you choose to lead.

4   Have you not made us
    partners in mission,
    loving as you love,
        walking your way?
    How shall we answer,
    knowing you call us?
    Yes, we will follow;
        we will obey.

Matthew 11:29; 28:19, 20; John 13:13; Philippians 1:21; 1 Peter 3:15; 1 John 2:6
Subject index: B.3, F.5, H.6
5 5 5 4 D
Suggested tune: *Bunessan*

49.   **True and living**

1   Jesus, true and living bread,
    we recall that final meal –
    cold betrayal, all too soon!
    Deadly conflict, all too real!
    As we meet, at your command,
    may our hungry souls be fed;
    give us holy nourishment,
    Jesus, true and living bread.

2   Jesus, true and living way,
    you embraced our mortal strife:
    died, the shepherd for the sheep;
    rose, the resurrection life!
    You are heaven's open door,
    light of God's eternal day,
    source of hope and joy and peace,
    Jesus, true and living way.

3   Jesus, true and living vine,
    you have taught us we depend
    on your death, your sacrifice,
    suffering Master, gracious Friend;
    as we meet, we bring you thanks
    for your blood, recalled with wine;
    satisfy our thirsty hearts,
    Jesus, true and living vine.

Matthew 26:20-29; Mark 14:18-25; Luke 1:78, 79; 22:19-21; John 6:35; 9:5;
10:7-11; 11:25; 13:13, 21; 14:6; 15:1, 5, 15, 18; Romans 14:17;
1 Corinthians 11:23-26; Ephesians 2:14; Colossians 1:27;
Hebrews 1:9; 2:14-18; 1 Peter 2:21; Revelation 4:1
Subject index: B.3, F.5, I.6
7 7 7 7 D
Suggested tune: *Aberystwyth*

50.   **Light a candle**

1   Light a candle, tend its flame;
     light a candle, say a prayer;
     nurture visions, joys, concerns
     other minds and hearts can share.

2   Light a candle – watch it burn,
     spent for those who need to see;
     parable of Jesus' way,
     showing what our lives should be.

3   Light a candle – let it blaze:
     sign of faith, though dark the night;
     symbol of our only hope:
     Jesus Christ, the world's true Light.

Matthew 5:14-16; 10:44, 45; 20:27, 28; John 1:9; 2 Corinthians 4:6;
Galatians 6:2, 5; Philippians 2:15
Subject index: B.1, H.3
7 7 7 7
Suggested tune: *Ephraim*

51.   Triumph adorns the sufferings

1   Long has it raged: a fight since time began,
    as rebel forces scorn the Maker's plan –
    but evil powers must yield to love's demands:
    the universe remains within God's hands.

2   For with this fearsome conflict at its height,
    God's Son was born on earth to take the fight;
    he gave himself in love, the crucified,
    disarming his opponents when he died.

3   Now by the cross his victory is complete:
    his foes must bow before his wounded feet
    and recognise his kingship stands assured
    through mortal anguish, patiently endured.

4   Though still the struggles rage, the day is won –
    triumph adorns the sufferings of the Son!
    Though scarred or wounded, we need not despair:
    both death and life with Christ are ours to share.

Romans 6:8; 1 Corinthians 15:25, 58; Galatians 2:20; Philippians 2:8-11;
Colossians 2:15; Hebrews 2:9; Revelation 1:18, 12:7
Subject index: B.5, I.4, J.1
10 10 10 10
Suggested tunes: *Go Forth*; *Gower Street Chapel*

52.   Brother, Saviour, Lord

1 Lord Christ, you honoured human flesh
   by sharing human birth;
   you truly felt the joys and strains
       of life on earth;
       we hear your call
   to walk the way you trod,
   embodying in daily life
   the holiness of God.

2 For we are rescued by your death,
   the sacrifice you made –
   our self-inflicted wounds are healed,
       our debts are paid.
       Now may your cross
   frame everything we do;
   our bodies, hearts and minds, our all,
   we freely give to you.

3 Lord Christ, you have renewed our hope
   by rising from the grave;
   your conquest rendered death itself
       a helpless slave!
       In you we trust;
   our future is secured:
   we too shall rise and live with you,
   our Brother, Saviour, Lord.

Deuteronomy 6:5; Isaiah 53:5, 6; Matthew 22:37; Mark 12:29, 30; John 1:14;
1 Corinthians 11:1; 15:22, 26; Galatians 6:14; Colossians 1:13; Hebrews 2:10, 11;
1 Peter 1:3, 15, 16; 1 John 2:6
Subject index: B.1, H.6, I.3
8 6 8 4 4 6 8 6

53.   Compassion and community

1   Lord Christ, you walked our dusty streets,
    shared human life and felt its strain,
    yet through the kindness of your touch
    brought hope and health for fear and pain.

2   From those you loved and named your friends,
    whose hearts responded to your call,
    you shaped a new community
    where each should serve and honour all.

3   Your death and rising from the grave
    brought power for broken lives made new
    to all who followed where you led –
    who took your word and proved it true.

4   Use us, Lord, as your hands, your voice,
    and reach beyond our lives, to bring
    compassion and community –
    the signs that you are Lord and King.

Matthew 8:2, 3; Mark 1:40-42; Luke 5:12, 13; John 13:14, 15; 15:15, 17; 20:21;
Acts 10:38; Romans 5:5; Ephesians 1:19, 20; Philippians 2:3
Subject index: B.3, I.4, J.1
8 8 8 8 (LM)
Suggested tune: *Gonfalon Royal*

54.   Faith

1   Lord, every day may we discern
        your steady, loving hand,
    then grasp, with eager faith, our role
        in all that you have planned;
        grant us the faith that takes
        the way of sacrifice –
    that follows Christ, though such a course
        exacts a heavy price.

2   If what you ask of us entails
        some unexpected way,
    give us continued diligence
        to listen and obey;
        when threats arouse alarm
        with danger lurking near,
    let faith be ours to face the test
        and triumph over fear.

3   Produce in us the faith that clings
        to your unchanging word,
    till you fulfil the promises
        that now remain deferred.
        For all that lies ahead
        unseen by human eyes,
    for all tomorrow's challenge brings,
        Lord, cause our faith to rise!

Psalm 56:3; Matthew 6:31-33; 17:20; Mark 4:40; Luke 12:28-31; Romans 1:5;
10:17; 2 Corinthians 4:13; Philippians 3:8-11; Colossians 1:23; Titus 1:2
Subject index: G.3, H.6
8 6 8 6 6 6 8 6 D
Suggested tune: *Zimbabwe* (John Bell)

55. Mercy

1 Lord, for our scarred world, rife with contradiction:
   where powerful leaders disregard conviction;
   where science lacks the heart to heal affliction;
      mercy! Have mercy, Lord.

2 When commerce knows no moral test or measure;
   when many toil, yet few have wealth to treasure;
   when conscience offers no restraint on pleasure:
      mercy! Have mercy, Lord.

3 If dreams of peace meet threats of confrontation;
   if hearts remain untouched by education;
   if there's no cost to prayerful adoration –
      mercy! Have mercy, Lord.

2 Samuel 24:24; 1 Chronicles 21:24; Psalm 120:6, 7; Amos 8:5, 6;
Matthew 20:25; Mark 10:42; Ephesians 4:18, 19; James 5:4, 5
Subject index: F.5, G.2, J.2
11 11 11 6
Suggested tune: *Christe Sanctorum*

56.   **Your will be done**

1   Lord, forgive! We have not grasped
the richness of your care –
how your love embraces all
and reaches everywhere.
Help us truly understand
all of life is in your hand:
    may your will be done on earth,
    and may your kingdom come.

2   Lord, forgive when we consent
to take the easy way
as we disregard your call
within the everyday.
Help us fashion all we do
to reflect our faith in you:
    may your will be done on earth,
    and may your kingdom come.

3   Lord, forgive: our minds are dull,
our hands and feet are slow;
we have seldom lived in ways
that helped your people grow.
Help us live as you intend,
as ambassadors you send:
    may your will be done on earth,
    and may your kingdom come.

Matthew 6:10; Luke 11:2; Acts 17:25-28; 2 Corinthians 5:20;
Philippians 2:12; Colossians 3:23; Hebrews 10:25
Subject index: G.2, I.2, J.1
7 6 7 6 7 7 7 6
Suggested tune: *Kelvingrove*

57.   Sure who I am

1   Lord, I thank you that I can be sure who I am:
    not in anxiously probing the depths of my soul,
    and not in the clutter of things I possess,
    for whatever I own, it cannot make me whole.

2   If a job I can do gives me some sense of worth,
    or the love of my family nurtures my heart,
    or if I have friends whom I treasure and trust –
    all of this can be fragile and soon fall apart.

3   Yet if all of my failures and faults weigh me down,
    and if all my achievements seem less than enough,
    I thank you I still can be sure who I am,
    for I'm known by you, held by you, safe in your love.

Psalm 27:10; Ecclesiastes 2:11; 4:4, 8; Jeremiah 17:9; Luke 12:15; John 10:28, 29;
Romans 7:21-24; Galatians 4:9; 1 Timothy 6:7, 17; 1 John 3:1
Subject index: F.4, G.1, H.2
12 12 11 12
Suggested tune: *Stowey*

58.   We will offer

1   Lord Jesus Christ, this world has lost its way;
     you call your church to mission day by day;
     so give us courage and the words to say –
         Lord, we will offer the news you give us.

2   When wealth abounds, yet billions have no share;
     when many starve, but very few will care;
     when bankrupt cultures echo with despair,
         Lord, we will offer the hope you give us.

3   When, deep inside, so many feel alone,
     and crave a home, a haven of their own;
     when passions flow, but kindness is unknown,
         Lord, we will offer the love you give us.

4   When war and terror leave their victims dead
     amid an age of hearts awash with dread,
     when people fear the days that lie ahead,
         Lord, we will offer the peace you give us.

Matthew 24:6-8; 28:18-20; Mark 16:15, 16; John 16:33; Acts 4:29;
Romans 5:5; 1 John 3:18
Subject index: G.2, H.7, J.1
10 10 10 10
Suggested tune: *Engleberg*, adapted

59. You offered full surrender

1   Lord Jesus, Living Word,
    in love you came to reach us;
    born one of us on earth,
    you spoke the truth to teach us;
        your deeds and words are one,
        your teaching and your living –
        such pure integrity,
        so righteous, so forgiving.

2   How graciously you dealt
    with all who came to hear you;
    how forceful your demands
    on those you gathered near you –
        but some who wielded power
        condemned you as mistaken,
        for by your faithful words
        the human heart is shaken.

3   You waited in the night,
    your earthly labours ended,
    prepared to meet your foes,
    whatever they intended –
        to all this world might do
        you offered full surrender:
        Lord, how it stirs our hearts,
        this hour that shows your splendour.

Matthew 26:45, 46; Mark 14:41, 42;
John 1:10-12; 6:68; 7:46; 17:2, 4, 5
Subject index: A.2, F.3
6 7 6 7 D
Suggested tune: *Vreuchten*

60. Teach me how to live

1 Lord Jesus, Teacher, speak:
  enable me to know,
  in all life's complex twists and turns,
  the way that I should go;

2 rekindle my resolve
  to follow you today,
  that I may share the joy of those
  who listen and obey;

3 and may your Spirit bring
  the wisdom that I seek
  for each decision, every choice
  that I shall make this week;

4 and may your word direct
  my plans throughout this year
  to focus chiefly on the things
  that show your kingdom near;

5 so listen to my prayer:
  to you, my God, I give
  my time, my dreams and energies –
  now teach me how to live!

Joshua 24:15; Isaiah 30:21; John 13:17; Ephesians 5:10; James 1:5
Subject index: B.3, F.5, H.6
6 6 8 6 (SM)
Suggested tune: *Sandys*

61. **Your living Word**

1 Lord of the word of life,
   Lord of the sacred page,
   bring us the truth we need
   now, in our troubled age:
   until we know our hearts have heard
   the voice of Christ, your living Word.

2 Open the ancient book,
   speak through it once again,
   making its meaning clear,
   making its challenge plain:

3 Draw out the prophets' words;
   use the translators' care;
   harness the scholars' skills;
   hear every preacher's prayer:

4 So may your Spirit's touch
   highlight our Saviour's way,
   helping us understand,
   prompting us to obey:

Deuteronomy 32:47; John 1:1, 14; 14:26; 16:33; 2 Timothy 2:15; 3:16, 17;
Hebrews 1:1; 4:12; James 1:22, 25
Subject index: E, F.5, H.1
6 6 6 6 refrain 8 8
Suggested tune: *Little Cornard*

62. Your Spirit's bubbling spring

1 Lord, you've invited us to come –
   you've heard our thirsty cry;
   fill us, so once again we know
   your Spirit's joyful overflow
   where now our hearts are dry.

2 Into our lives you speak the truth –
   eternal seed is sown!
   May this enduring treasure stored
   in our hearts honour you, our Lord,
   through lives that make you known.

3 May we be rooted, deep and sure,
   in you, our gracious King;
   now, through our timid souls reveal
   the flowing power of love made real,
   your Spirit's bubbling spring.

4 Give us a clearer sight of heaven
   to captivate our gaze:
   how, with that vast, uncounted throng,
   we too will share the joyful song
   of everlasting praise.

Isaiah 58:1; Luke 6:43-45; John 7:37, 38;
Colossians 2:7; Revelation 7:9, 15, 16
Subject index: D, F.5, H.4
8 6 8 8 6
Suggested tune: *Gatescarth*

63.   Majestic humility

1   Majestic humility: God came to earth,
    unequalled his greatness, unnoticed his birth;
    his boyhood informed by the law's rich demands
    till faith found a shape through a carpenter's hands.

2   Majestic humility: home left behind,
    he took to the roads, so that others could find
    the care of a Father who loved them so much,
    explained in his teaching, affirmed in his touch.

3   Majestic humility: yielding his will,
    Christ went in obedience to Calvary's hill:
    all our guilty burdens he there made his own
    with thorns for his crown and with wood for his throne.

4   Majestic humility: endless his reign –
    but always the scars from those sufferings remain.
    No love that we offer, no worship we bring
    discharges our debt to our Saviour and King.

Matthew 11:28, 29; 26:39; Mark 1:14; 14:36; Luke 2:51, 52; 12:32; 22:42;
John 1:11, 14; 16:27; 20:20; 1 Peter 2:24; Revelation 5:6
Subject index: A.3, F.2
11 11 11 11
Suggested tune: *St Denio*

64. My love, my worship

1   Most holy God, beyond all mortal sight,
    draw near and turn my inmost darkness bright
    until my soul, with trembling and delight,
        is led to worship.

2   Reveal the truth, and captivate my mind;
    all falsehood I am glad to leave behind;
    and as I seek your face, Lord, may I find
        the path to worship.

3   Give me a vision of your glorious throne,
    a glimpse of endless beauty there made known –
    there purge my hopes and dreams, that you alone
        shall have my worship.

4   In your love is the power that makes me new,
    the guardian and the guide of all I do;
    with gratitude I offer back to you
        my love, my worship.

5   So may I walk the true disciple's way
    of eagerness to listen and obey,
    my will aligned to yours as, day by day,
        I bow in worship.

Isaiah 6:1; John 4:24; 14:23; 15:10; Romans 5:5; 1 Timothy 6:16
Subject index: A.3, F.5, H.4
10 10 10 5
Suggested tune: *Engleberg*

65.   May all I do

1   My God, I ask with gratitude and joy:
    may you be pleased with how I live today.
    The highest of my heart's desires remains
    to make you glad by all I do and say.

2   Without your gift of wisdom I shall fail,
    so may your Spirit's prompting be my cue,
    and may the clear instruction of your word
    remind me daily how to follow you.

3   In every motive, attitude and thought,
    may holy fear inspire integrity,
    producing victories won in heart and mind,
    a sacred offering you alone will see.

4   May all I do be done for your delight,
    and not for honours I could call my own;
    let servanthood become my way of life,
    to make your perfect love more clearly known.

Psalms 19:14; 119:9, 10; Matthew 20:26-28; Mark 10:43, 44; 2 Corinthians 10:5;
Ephesians 5:10; Philippians 2:5-7; James 1:5; 1 John 3:16-18
Subject index: F.5, H.6
10 10 10 10
Suggested tune: *Chilton Foliat*

66. Your captivating love for me

1   My God, within your love I find
a sense of worth unknown before:
for you, the gracious Holy One,
have made me yours for evermore.

2   Your full acceptance opens wide
the door to real security:
in spite of all that I have done
you love me unreservedly.

3   The safety of your care promotes
the peace I need to make me whole:
a blazing spark of gratitude
begins to flame within my soul.

4   Your captivating love for me
has undermined this world's allure;
for nothing rivals knowing Christ,
who died to make the guilty pure.

5   Remade, forgiven, reconciled,
my all to you I gladly give,
as I explore the path of love,
the way that I was made to live.

John 6:37; 2 Corinthians 5:17, 18; Ephesians 1:4, 5; Philippians 3:7-9; 4:7;
1 Timothy 1:16; 1 John 2:15; 3:1; 4:16, 18-20
Subject index: A.4, F.2, G.1
8 8 8 8 (LM)
Suggested tune: *Church Triumphant*

67. Bring my all

1   My Lord, I bring my all to you:
    my hopes and dreams; the plans I make;
    my pains and pleasures, thoughts and words,
    and each decision I must take;
    my energies, and every skill –
    Lord, redirect them as you will.

2   My time is yours, and all I do:
    the duties that consume my days;
    the unknown possibilities
    along uncharted future ways;
    to you I owe my every breath:
    my time is yours, from now till death.

3   But knowing I am deeply flawed,
    my God, into your hands I give
    the habits and the weaknesses
    that undermine the way I live,
    the shame that lingers through the years,
    the secret doubts and lurking fears.

4   Lord, everything I am is yours,
    and everything that I possess,
    for you held nothing back for me:
    how could I offer any less?
    Your cross still speaks; I hear your call –
    my Lord, I bring to you my all.

Psalm 31:15; Proverbs 3:6; 16:3; Mark 12:30; Romans 5:8; 8:32; 12:1;
James 3:2; 4:13-15; 1 Peter 5:7; 1 John 1:10
Subject index: F.5, G.3, H.4
8 8 8 8 8 8
Suggested tune: *Abingdon*

68. No power

1 No power can drain the Christian's joy –
   our trust is in the living Lord.
      Through days beset by searing grief
      that strains the sinews of belief,
   the joy of God runs deeper still:
   in Christ our safety is assured.

2 No power can crush the Christian's life
   though untold trials are close at hand –
      when pressures crowd and troubles grow,
      when fierce afflictions bring us low,
   God shows his splendour through our lives
   and gives us faith and grace to stand.

3 No power can touch the Christian's Lord:
   no more is Christ held in the tomb!
      The Son of Man, once crucified,
      who seemed defeated when he died,
   was raised by God to endless life –
   this Easter news dispels our gloom!

4 No power can quench the Christian's hope:
   the words of Jesus still stand fast,
      for he has promised to prepare
      a glorious place for us to share,
   where we shall see him face to face
   and find ourselves at home, at last.

John 14:1-3; Romans 8:35-39; 1 Corinthians 15:20;
2 Corinthians 4:7-10; 13:4; 1 Peter 1:6, 8, 9
Subject index: B.5, G.3, J.4
8 8 8 8 8 8
Suggested tune: *Melita*

69.   I thank you, Lord

1   Once I was far, so far from you,
    my thoughts confused, my worth unclear;
        I thank you, Lord, that you reached out;
        you grasped my hand and drew me near.

2   Once life was dark, beset by gloom –
    a shadow-land where all was night.
        I thank you, Lord, you rescued me
        and brought me back into the light.

3   Once life was bleak without your love –
    instead of hope, the taste of death;
        I thank you, Lord, for joy renewed
        since you gave me your living breath.

4   Once I was lost – I sought in vain
    some friendly face, some homely sound;
        I thank you, Lord, you called my name:
        because you care, now I am found.

Isaiah 43:1; Romans 5:5; Ephesians 2:13; Colossians 1:13; 1 Peter 5:7
Subject index: F.4, G.1, H.1
8 8 8 8 (LM)
Suggested tune: *O Waly Waly*

70.   Daily we live

1   One sacrifice, both perfect and complete:
    Christ gave his life to do the Father's will.
    Now by his death our sins are all forgiven –
    those long forgotten, those which haunt us still –
    each one the Lord has promised to forget:
    no longer need we bear that heavy debt.

2   Daily we die, releasing from our grasp
    this fading world with its beguiling toys;
    daily we take the cross to be our own,
    drawn by the foretaste of eternal joys.
    Greater by far than what we leave behind
    are all the treasures which in Christ we find.

3   Daily we live as citizens of heaven,
    eager to reach the goal and win the prize:
    earthly ambitions now attract us less;
    broad new horizons open to our eyes.
    May we be always worthy of the call
    to serve as partners with the Lord of all.

4   Should we attempt to give what he deserves,
    all that we have would simply not suffice;
    yet he delights in humble, trusting hearts,
    yielded to be a living sacrifice.
    Won by his love, with gratitude we bring
    our daily lives to Christ, our Lord and King.

Psalm 32:1; Isaiah 57:15; Jeremiah 31:34; Micah 6:8; Matthew 16:24;
Mark 8:34; Luke 9:23; Romans 12:1; 2 Corinthians 4:17, 18; 5:19;
Ephesians 4:1; Philippians 3:7, 8, 13, 14, 20; Colossians 1:14;
Hebrews 8:12; 10:7, 12, 14; 1 John 4:19
Subject index: B.4, H.1, J.4
10 10 10 10 10 10
Suggested tune: *Yorkshire (Stockport)*

71.   **Voice of hope**

1   Our ears have heard the voice of hope,
     for you have dared to walk this earth,
     have shared the strains of human life
     and died, enabling our rebirth.

2   Our hearts have felt the warmth of hope,
     the tender touch that proves your care:
     you reached inside our broken lives
     and snapped the shackles of despair.

3   Our eyes have seen the signs of hope
     where you restore the fractured soul,
     rekindle love and dignity
     and render broken friendships whole.

4   Then make us, Lord, a voice of hope
     for every street and every home,
     to spread the vision on your heart
     and work to see your kingdom come.

Hosea 6:1, 2; 14:4; Matthew 9:38; 28:19; Mark 16:15; Romans 5:5; 8;
2 Corinthians 5:17; Galatians 2:16; 5:1; Ephesians 2:15-17
Subject index: H.6, I.2, J.1
8 8 8 8 (LM)
Suggested tune: *Duke Street*

72.   Reshaping twisted lives

1   Our eyes have seen how you can take life's worst
         and build life's best:
             though hardship, war or pain
             cast shadows on our days,
             your promise brings us hope
             no darkness can erase;
     your peace enfolds us – Lord, how can we fail
         to be impressed?

2   Our ears have heard of those whom you reclaimed
         from great despair;
             in Christ you bore our shame
             and shared our deepest loss –
             we find our bleakest tales
             rewritten at his cross
     as beauty, birthed in wretchedness and grief,
         proclaims your care.

3   Our hearts have felt the gentleness and warmth
         that mean so much:
             for you see all our faults
             yet name us as your own,
             reshaping twisted lives
             to make your splendour known –
     how deep, how rich and lasting are the joys
         in lives you touch.

4   Receive our praise: for all that we have felt,
         have seen or heard!
             Amazed at how your grace
             makes broken people new,
             how glad we are to bring
             our worship, Lord, to you –
     the joyful shouts and grateful sighs of hearts
         your love has stirred.

Romans 5:3-5; 8:28-30, 35-37
Subject index: F.4, H.1, I.2
10 4 6 6 6 6 10 4
Suggested tune: *Luckington*

73. Fulcrum of the age

1 Pause here a while and contemplate
   our story's central page,
   the turning point of history's tale,
   the fulcrum of the age.

2 The prophets find enacted here
   the visions they foresaw;
   here, too, are met the full demands
   of Israel's ancient law.

3 The suffering servant of the Lord
   here gulps his final breath –
   for this world's powers here crucify
   the Man from Nazareth.

4 Here must the march of history wait,
   constrained by Love's commands:
   earth's proudest empires fall to dust;
   Love's righteous verdict stands.

5 And each of us is offered here
   forgiveness and new birth,
   a place within the coming age,
   the remade heavens and earth.

6 Pause here with joyful gratitude:
   the cross spells hope restored.
   Here God is making all things new
   in Jesus Christ our Lord.

Isaiah 52:14; Daniel 2:44; Matthew 5:17; 16:21; Mark 9:31; Luke 9:22, 44;
John 3:16-21, 36; Acts 2:38, 39; Galatians 4:4, 5; 1 Peter 1:10-12; Revelation 21:5
Subject index: B.4, F.2, J.1
8 6 8 6 (CM)
Suggested tune: *St Peter*

74. Proclaim the death

1 Proclaim the death of Christ the Lord:
a man betrayed, unfairly tried,
then – by colluding earthly powers –
condemned and promptly crucified.

2 Proclaim the death of Christ the Lord,
where hope and promise meet at last
with prophets' dreams and priestly rites
in Christ fulfilled, by Christ surpassed.

3 Proclaim the death of Christ the Lord,
the monstrous cost of full release,
as God affirms, by bread and wine:
our rebel hearts are offered peace.

4 Proclaim the death of Christ the Lord
and make his resurrection known
till history's glorious goal is reached:
the rightful King ascends his throne.

Luke 24:44; Acts 2:23; 7:52; 1 Corinthians 11:23-26; 15:3, 4;
2 Corinthians 1:20; Hebrews 2:8, 9; 1 Peter 1:10-12, 18, 19
Subject index: B.4, G.2, I.6
8 8 8 8 (LM)
Suggested tune: *Melcombe*

75.   Our lasting joy and our grateful song

1   Sing of the God whose love gave the cosmos birth;
    sing of the God whose power shaped a fruitful earth.
    Think of the distant stars, by human eyes unseen;
    think of the springtime leaves that are fresh and green.
        This is our lasting joy and our grateful song:
        our Creator is good; he is wise and strong.

2   Sing of the God whose love sets our hearts ablaze!
    Sing of the God whose gifts undergird our days.
    Look at creation's wealth; God simply loves to give,
    amply providing all that we need to live.
        This is our lasting joy and our grateful song:
        for his generous care lasts a whole life long.

3   Sing of the God whose love is in Christ made known;
    sing of the God who calls us to be his own.
    Pardon for all our sin, hope to dispel our fear –
    Jesus, who died and rose, makes the promise clear.
        This is our lasting joy and our grateful song:
        how secure is God's love, where we now belong.

Genesis 1; Psalms 104:14; 136:1, 4, 5, 9; Isaiah 43:1; 46:3, 4; Luke 24:47;
John 15:16; Romans 5:1, 2; 1 Timothy 6:17; 1 John 3:1, 16; 4:18
Subject index: A.4, F.3, H.2
11 11 12 11 11 11
Suggested tune: *Water End*

76. Bring words and music

1   Sing praise to God! How good it is, and right
        to turn our thoughts and hearts to him in praise;
    bring words and music for the Lord's delight.

2   Creation shows his majesty and might –
        what beauty all his handiwork displays!
    Sing praise to God! How good it is, and right.

3   Exalt our God: our Life, our Hope, our Light,
        whose loving-kindness sets our hearts ablaze:
    bring words and music for the Lord's delight.

4   Let worship echo through the darkest night
        and be the steady pulse of all our days;
    sing praise to God! How good it is, and right.

5   Then banish anger, jealousy and spite,
        and hear the call the faithful heart obeys:
    bring words and music for the Lord's delight.

6   Let every voice and instrument unite,
        each skilful tune and finely crafted phrase:
    sing praise to God! How good it is, and right;
    bring words and music for the Lord's delight.

Psalms 19:1; 27:1; 33:1-3; 34:1; 92:1; 134:1; Lamentations 3:22; Ephesians 4:31
Subject index: A.1, F.3, H.6
10 10 10

Inclusive language variations
verse 1, line 2: to turn our thoughts and hearts to God in praise;
verse 2, line 1: Creation shows such majesty and might –
verse 2, line 2: what beauty all God's handiwork displays!

77. **Someone told me**

1 Someone told me of a Saviour
who had died to rescue me,
paid my debt and won my freedom
at a place called Calvary.
 Thank you, Lord, that someone told me
 how your love has dealt with sin –
 help me pass the news to others,
 those you long to gather in.

2 Someone came from somewhere distant
to this unknown, foreign place,
bore the cost of opposition
for the kingdom ruled by grace.
 Thank you, Lord, that someone travelled
 so the gospel could take root
 and, within this land and culture,
 bear a crop of lasting fruit.

3 Someone toiled to share the Scriptures,
worked with diligence and skill –
now I read what they translated,
hear your voice and learn your will.
 Thank you, Lord, that someone studied –
 let my grateful heart be stirred;
 through my words and in my actions
 help my neighbours catch your word.

4 Someone took the time to show me
what it means to walk with you –
how the lifelong call to follow
must determine all I do.
 Thank you, Lord, that someone nurtured,
 helped me follow and obey;
 form in me a good example
 of your true and living way.

John 3:16; Acts 1:8; Romans 15:20; 1 Corinthians 11:1;
Galatians 2:20; Hebrews 13:7, 8
Subject index: G.3, H.1, I.4
8 7 8 7 D
Suggested tunes: Unnamed tune by Paul Drinkwater; *Abbots Leigh*

78.   Sprinkle me

1   Sprinkle me with water
    till my heart is clean;
    lift my guilty burdens,
    all I've done and been.

2   Soak away the hardness
    from my heart of stone;
    by your gracious handling
    make your mercy known.

3   Keep me always mindful
    how this walk began –
    faith's unfolding journey
    with the Son of Man.

4   Through the heat of battle
    shield me by your power,
    till the great fulfilment
    of the final hour.

5   Till then, may I serve you
    everywhere I go;
    through my daily living
    let your water flow.

Psalm 51:9; Ezekiel 36:25, 26; John 7:38; Colossians 3:17; 1 Peter 1:4, 5
Subject index: F.6, H.6, I.5
6 5 6 5
Suggested tune: *Gott ein Vater*

79.   Teach us

1   Teach us to know your heart –
mercy's unfailing beat;
welcoming, open arms;
love that is made complete,
    where your forgiveness makes it plain
    that all are free to start again.

2   Teach us to seek your will –
all that is just and right;
may all our days be spent
consciously in your sight.
    Lord, may your holy care shine through
    in all we are, and say, and do.

3   Teach us to walk your way –
humbly to seek your face,
God of unequalled power,
God of unending grace.
    May we show, with integrity,
    the imprint of eternity.

Micah 6:8; Matthew 5:16; John 8:11; Ephesians 5:10
Subject index: A.3, H.4, J.1
6 6 6 6 8 8
Suggested tune: *Little Cornard*

80. Teach us to walk

1   Teach us to walk at a pace of your choosing,
    urged by your voice, or restrained by your hand,
    catching the rhythms of life you intended,
    shaped to the patterns you've lovingly planned.

2   Teach us to walk on the road where you lead us,
    conscious we travel with you at our side;
    help us to focus our daily decisions,
    making your kingdom our work and our guide.

3   Teach us to walk in the strength of your Spirit,
    filled with your wisdom and fed by your word;
    fire us with passion for Christlike obedience,
    turning to action the truth that we've heard.

4   Teach us to walk to the goal you determine –
    open eternity's view to our eyes,
    until we live by that broader perspective,
    hearing your call as our purpose and prize.

Psalm 16:8; Isaiah 40:29-31; Matthew 4:4; 6:33; 11:28-30; John 13:17;
Ephesians 5:1, 10; Philippians 3:13, 14; Titus 2:14; James 1:5, 22
Subject index: F.5, G.3, H.6
11 10 11 10
Suggested tune: *Epiphany Hymn*

81. The voice of God

1 The ancient prophets searched for Christ –
those saints from Israel's past;
across a thousand years and more,
a dream, a hope they dimly saw
of one who'd come at last.

2 And then he came: a child, a man,
a voice, a human face:
through stories told and bodies healed
his life and death and life revealed
the rescue of our race.

3 And those with whom he'd shared his years
recorded all they'd known
to spread the message far and wide:
the living Lord, the One who'd died,
now calls us as his own.

4 Where hearts and ears are open, still
Christ's Spirit brings his word:
the light of truth, the written page,
and in our lives, our world, our age,
the voice of God is heard.

Numbers 24:17; Matthew 20:28; Mark 10:45; Luke 1:1-4; 19:10; John 1:14;
16:12-14; Acts 10:38, 39; 1 Corinthians 2:10-13; Galatians 4:4; Hebrews 4:12;
1 Peter 1:10, 11; 1 John 1:1-3; Revelation 1:18; 2:29; 3:13, 22
Subject index: B.3, E
8 6 8 8 6
Suggested tune: *Repton*

82.   You love us

1   The beauty of your holiness
    outshines the brightest star –
    Lord, who can bear your scrutiny?
    You see us as we are!
        Yet all the faults we try to hide
        or, stung by shame, confess –
        not one of these, however bad,
        could make you love us less.

2   No gift of ours could be enough:
    what can we do or say
    to match the kindness and the care
    you show us day by day?
        No hymn we sing, no fervent prayer,
        no rite enshrined in law,
        no labour, vow or sacrifice
        could make you love us more!

Deuteronomy 7:7, 8; Psalms 15:1; 103:3, 8-10; Isaiah 64:6; Jeremiah 17:9, 10;
31:3; Lamentations 3:22, 23; Micah 6:6, 7; Ephesians 2:8, 9
Subject index: F.4, G.1, I.2
8 6 8 6 D (DCM)
Suggested tune: *Kingsfold*

83.   Death and life

1   The call of Christ is death and life:
    to find through pain and loss
    the resurrection power he gives
    to those who share his cross.

2   And if, through all the trials of faith,
    we patiently endure,
    then we shall share his joyful reign:
    his promise stands secure.

3   And yet, in clear and solemn terms
    he makes the warning known
    that those who have denied his name
    he will not call his own.

4   If faith should falter, still our Lord
    is with us to the end:
    through all our weakness, Christ remains
    our true and faithful friend.

5   Lord Christ, you see our fragile faith,
    our hopes of staying true;
    then give us patience, joy and strength –
    the grace to walk with you.

Matthew 10:32, 33; 16:24, 25; 28:20; Mark 8:34, 35; Luke 9:23, 24; 12:8, 9;
2 Timothy 2:11-13; Hebrews 13:5; Revelation 2:26
Subject index: B.4, H.4
8 6 8 6 (CM)
Suggested tune: *Irish*

84.   **Render what is God's**

1   The call of Jesus Christ rings clear:
to render what is God's to God.
Yet all the world belongs to him,
   and as his own he names it;
the life that we assume is ours,
   in kingly power he claims it.

2   Lord Jesus, we must offer you
the gifts which you gave first to us,
our wealth, our talents and our time:
   you meant these gifts for sharing,
for showing love and spreading grace,
   creating, serving, caring.

3   Though all we are, or have, or give
falls so far short, so very far,
of everything that you deserve,
   may you, in love, still treasure
whatever gifts we humbly bring
   for your eternal pleasure.

4   May all our strength and all our skill
be honed and tuned for your delight,
reflecting clearly, hour by hour,
   the debt of grace we owe you:
Lord Jesus, use our daily lives
   to help your world to know you.

1 Chronicles 29:14; Psalm 24:1; Matthew 22:21, 37; Mark 12:17, 30, 31;
Luke 17:10; 20:25; 1 Corinthians 4:7; 12:7; 1 Peter 2:12
Subject index: B.3, F.4, H.4
8 8 8 7 8 7

85.   Artistic skill

1   The crispness of a frosty winter day;
the warm caressing of a summer breeze;
the beauty of the flowers announcing spring;
the multicoloured cloaks of autumn trees;

2   the open vastness of a cloudless sky;
the swirling stars, a billion points of light;
the crashing of a wave along the shore;
the outline of a jagged mountain height;

3   the slow, insistent drumming of the rain;
the melodies of birdsong heard at dawn;
the soft, contented purring of a cat;
the crying of a baby, newly-born;

4   the lasting firmness of a grassy hill;
the roughness and the subtle strength of wood;
the piercing chill of iron, cold and sharp;
the tenderness of love in pulsing blood –

5   creative and imaginative God,
whose word gave shape and life to all we see,
in breathless hush at your artistic skill
we wait to hear what you want us to be.

Genesis 1; Psalm 8:3, 4; Proverbs 8:22-35; Ephesians 5:10; 1 John 4:10
Subject index: A.2, E, H.1
10 10 10 10
Suggested tune: *West Ashton*

86. Sabbath

1 The flow of time is pulsing
to rhythms God has made –
in days and nights and seasons
life's pattern is displayed.
The Sabbath in the old way,
the Lord's Day in the new,
are meant as time to ponder
the things we know are true.

2 This solemn time for leisure,
this joyful break, is given
by God who laboured six days
and rested one in seven;
yet life's relentless pressures
now threaten heaven's best,
this time when all may worship,
this time when all may rest.

3 This pause in life's endeavours
provides a time to care
for neighbours, near or distant,
and one good earth we share;
a time to let compassion
displace relentless greed,
as joy in God's abundance
restores the hope we need.

4 May God, whose holy presence
pervades both time and space,
disrupt the frantic jarring
of life's aggressive pace;
may he renew our vision
till wholeness is restored,
with love and justice kindled
in honour of the Lord!

Genesis 1:14; 2:2, 3; Exodus 20:8-11; Deuteronomy 5:12-14; Isaiah 56:1, 2;
58:13, 14; Mark 2:27; Hebrews 4:9; Revelation 1:10
Subject index: A.5, I.2, J.1
7 6 7 6 D
Suggested tune: *Salley Gardens*

87.   **You have fed us**

1   The journey is too far for us –
we lack sufficient strength
to travel, day by day, a path
of unknown future length;
    but you have fed us bread and wine
    to help us persevere:
    a joyful, step-by-step advance,
    in faith and not in fear.

2   The battle is too fierce for us:
we hear the hostile sound
of blatant lies, of subtle threats,
of hatred all around;
    but you have fed us bread and wine
    as on the night you made
    your journey to Gethsemane –
    the night you were betrayed.

3   The darkness is too deep for us –
the sense of closing day,
the lostness of a broken world,
the symptoms of decay;
    but you have fed us bread and wine
    and named us salt and light,
    the messengers of truth and hope
    throughout this dark world's night.

4   The labour is too much for us –
the hungry we should feed,
the lonely, sick, oppressed and poor –
an endless sea of need;
    but you have fed us bread and wine
    and with this holy meal
    equipped our hearts for servanthood,
    the life of faith made real.

1 Kings 19:7; Psalms 12:2; 120:2; Matthew 5:13-16; 25:34-36; Mark 6:32-37;
John 9:4; 13:14-16; 15:18, 19; 1 Corinthians 11:23-25; 2 Corinthians 5:7;
Ephesians 5:8-12; 6:12; Hebrews 12:2; 13:6; James 4:14
Subject index: F.5, H.8, I.6
8 6 8 6 D (DCM)
Suggested tune: *Vox Dilecti*

88. Holy fools

1 The One we follow gladly chose
 a way that few think wise –
 a way whose merit human minds
 are slow to recognise.

2 His suffering love, his gentle path,
 leave pomp and power behind,
 and render this world's futile dreams
 exposed and undermined.

3 Too narrow is this foolish path
 for vanity and pride –
 they shrivel under scrutiny
 from Christ, the crucified.

4 Christ's servants often stand disguised
 as jesters, clowns or fools,
 who still pursue the game of life,
 but play by different rules.

5 A holy fool's prophetic voice
 can shine a shaft of light;
 a clown, releasing joy and tears,
 enables clearer sight.

6 Christ calls us to embrace this way
 that many still despise;
 for those disdained as holy fools
 are honoured in his eyes.

Matthew 7:13, 14; 11:28, 29; 20:28; Mark 10:45;
1 Corinthians 1:20, 21, 27, 28; 2:6-10; 3:18, 19; 4:10
Subject index: B.3, H.6, I.4
8 6 8 6
Suggested tune: *St Bernard*

89.   The God of peace

1   The peace of God be with you
   to answer all your fear,
   to calm your anxious feelings
   and keep your thinking clear;
   the peace of God be with you
   to underline his care,
   whose eager ears are open
   to trusting, thankful prayer –
     this peace our God has promised
     will more than satisfy
     the aching human hunger
     for understanding 'why'.

2   The God of peace be with you,
   who names you as his own
   and calls you to the lifestyle
   his faithful saints have shown;
   the God of peace be with you
   to nurture your delight
   and focus your attention
   on what is true and right;
     till, as his Spirit kindles
     new visions to pursue,
     God's presence, peace and purpose
     bring joy to all you do.

Philippians 4:5-9
Subject index: F.5, G.1, H.2
7 6 7 6 Triple
Suggested tune: *Thaxted*

Inclusive language variations
verse 1, lines 6-7: to underline the care
                    of eager ears, receptive
verse 2, line 2:   who names you as Christ's own
verse 2, line 4:   that faithful saints have shown;
verse 2, line 9:   till, as the Spirit kindles

90.   Creation's disarray

1 The summer cools and fades;
   the fallen leaves decay;
   they nurture growth that signals spring,
   a brighter coming day.

2 Life's fragile web demands
   a balanced interplay
   of flora, fauna, climate, land,
   of predator and prey.

3 But now creation groans
   in turmoil and dismay,
   with broken landscapes, mutant cells
   and genes that go astray.

4 Disaster and disease
   still threaten and betray
   the dreams and hopes of those who feel
   creation's disarray.

5 Yet Christ has felt these strains
   that mar our mortal way;
   his death and rising point towards
   a brighter future day.

6 Renew creation, Lord!
   Let death no more hold sway.
   Set all the cosmos free at last
   in your eternal day.

Genesis 8:22; Psalm 104:20, 21; Ecclesiastes 3:1, 2; Romans 8:19-22;
1 Corinthians 15:20-23; Hebrews 2:17
Subject index: A.2, F.5, J.4
6 6 8 6 (SM)
Suggested tune: *St Thomas*

91. When Christ arose

1 They had wondered who would move the stone – but
    found the stone had gone;
they were looking for a body in the tomb, but there was none;
they had come to mourn a dead man but they met the
    Risen One
on the day when Christ arose.

2 Her companions left the tomb, but Mary lingered there,
    and cried;
she had trusted in the Master – but then he was crucified;
so she failed to recognise him – but it thrilled her deep inside
when he gently spoke her name.

3 And two others – who had heard but not believed – that
    very day
met the Lord, but did not know him as they walked along
    the way;
and he made to journey on, but they persuaded him to stay –
when he broke the bread, they knew!

4 Through a long but fruitless night some trawled the
    Galilean lake
till a kind but unknown voice advised a different way to take:
then their catch was so immense, their nets were filled,
    but did not break –
and the stranger was the Lord.

5 Have we, too, not bowed in worship, but with lurking doubt
    and fear?
And have we not heard his call, but known obedience may
    cost dear?
Let us go – but in the confidence his Spirit has come near –
Christ is Lord, is Lord of all!

Matthew 28:17, 18; Mark 16:3, 4; Luke 14:33; 24:1-3, 13-16, 28-32;
John 20:10, 11, 13, 14; 21:1-4, 7, 11; Acts 1:8; Romans 5:5
Subject index: B.5, F.5, H.7
15 15 15 7
Suggested tune: *Vision*

92.   God has come to earth

1   To Abram came a promise
    he strained to understand:
    a family of nations,
    an unknown, distant land.
    In resolute obedience
    his pilgrim trek began;
    his faith became the channel
    for God's unfolding plan.

2   When Israel's sons and daughters
    were trapped in slavery,
    God sent them a deliverer
    who led the people free;
    but since the Lord is holy
    he set his law in place
    to shape their life and culture,
    to show their need for grace.

3   In later generations
    the people craved a king,
    and spurned the wise forewarning
    of pain this choice would bring;
    yet still God spoke to David
    and made his promise known:
    for one of his descendants,
    an everlasting throne.

4   God's Spirit guided history
    in ways no words can tell
    through monarchy and exile,
    as empires rose and fell;
    and in the prayerful musings
    of sages and of seers
    the outline of the promise
    grew sharper through the years.

5   What patience and what purpose!
Then, when the time was right,
the Child was born to Mary:
God's Son, our Life, our Light!
Beyond all expectation
this lowly human birth
brought God among his people:
our God has come to earth!

Genesis 12:1-4; Exodus 3:7-10; Leviticus 11:44, 45; 1 Samuel 8; 2 Samuel 7:16;
Psalm 132:11, 12; Matthew 1:23; Luke 1:35; 2:5-7; John 1:4, 14; Galatians 4:4
Subject index: A.4, I.2, J.1
7 6 7 6 D
Suggested tune: *Ellacombe*

93. **Prophet, Priest and King**

1 To Jerusalem he rides –
hear those loud hosannas ring!
Crowds acclaim him Son of David,
holy prophet, promised king.

2 He discerns the coming storm,
knows contention looms ahead:
rulers who reject his teaching
want this awkward prophet dead.

3 Soon upon a brutal cross
he will take his dying breath:
he, the priest, and he, the offering,
willingly embracing death.

4 Yet that cross was not the end:
he is risen! Death is slain!
So the king whom God appointed
comes to his eternal reign.

5 From the new Jerusalem
hear those alleluias ring!
Hail the gentle Man of Sorrows,
Christ, the Prophet, Priest and King!

Isaiah 53:3; Matthew 16:21; 20:17-19; 21:7-9, 27:30; Mark 8:31; 10:32-34;
11:7-10; 15:24, 37; Luke 9:22; 18:31-33; 19:35-38; 23:33, 46; 24:19, 26;
John 11:47-50; 12:12-15, 20-27; 1 Corinthians 15:20, 24-26;
Hebrews 8:1; 9:12; 10:12; Revelation 17:14; 19:1
Subject index: B.1, J.4
7 7 8 7

94. **Unlock my emotions**

1   Unlock my emotions: Lord, help me to feel
the depth of the love which your sufferings reveal;
unlock my emotions until I can see
the breadth of this love you have lavished on me.

2   Unlock my emotions: I need to release
the turmoil that hinders the flow of your peace;
unlock my emotions, those moments of fear
when I fail to lean on your pledge to be near.

3   Unlock my emotions and cause me to learn
your fervent compassion, your timeless concern.
Unlock my emotions for sensing the cost
of loving a world that is wilfully lost.

4   Unlock my emotions: Lord, help me to share
your love, which runs deeper than untold despair;
unlock my emotions: in my heart make real
the mingling of anguish and joy which you feel.

Romans 5:1, 5, 8; 8:37-39; 2 Corinthians 5:14, 15; Ephesians 3:19;
Hebrews 13:5, 6; 1 John 3:1; 4:10, 18
Subject index: F.5, G.1, H.1
11 11 11 11
Suggested tune: *St Denio*

95.   Sacred mystery

1   Unveil again your holy mystery –
    so shall our hungry hearts be fed;
    show us your blood within this wine, Lord;
    show us your body through this bread.

2   Open our hearts to feel the friendship
    shared in that hidden supper-room;
    sharpen our spirits to the dangers
    waiting and watching in the gloom.

3   Help us to understand what pressures
    drove your disciples' desperate flight;
    teach us to recognise the burden
    you made your own that dreadful night.

4   As we recall your mortal anguish –
    thorn-crown and cross-beam, nails and spear –
    show us the breadth of separation:
    God far from God, to bring us near!

5   Gather us in the sacred mystery
    where faith is nurtured and made strong:
    where bread speaks healing and forgiveness,
    where wine assures us we belong.

Matthew 26:20-29, 36-47, 55, 56; Mark 14:17-25, 32-44, 49-50; Luke 22:15-23,
39-48; 23:33; John 15:14; 18:1-3; 19:16-18; 1 Corinthians 11:23-26
Subject index: B.4, I.6
9 8 9 8
Suggested tune: *Spiritus Vitae*

96. The true and rightful King

1   We praise our God: the one who spoke of freedom,
whose promise still resounds from ages past:
his strength wrought Israel's exodus from Egypt;
his prophets' words have been fulfilled at last.
    We praise our Lord, the faithful Suffering Servant,
    whose life was all that Israel failed to be:
    who walked the path of pain and deepest darkness
    and by those sufferings set his people free.

2   We praise our God: the one who lives among us,
as once he did in Israel's desert day:
his towering fire to summon their obedience,
his towering cloud to guide them on their way.
    We praise our Lord, the child whom Mary carried,
    our Saviour, sharing human flesh and blood:
    the living Temple and the gentle Shepherd,
    the gracious Word that tells us God is good.

3   We praise our God: the one at work in history,
who chose and called a nation as his own;
who gave his law to shape a priestly people
whose holy lives could make his goodness known.
    We praise our Lord, who calls us to his service –
    to take his love, his message, everywhere;
    so shall the church of Christ, through joy and struggle,
    fulfil the calling all God's children share.

4   We praise our God: the one who is victorious,
who will not rest till justice is complete,
till hopes fulfilled surpass our deepest longings
and evil finds its ultimate defeat.
    We praise our Lord, who faced the fiercest battle,
    who tasted death for us, and drew its sting:
    so comes the day all powers, on earth, in heaven,
    acknowledge Christ the true and rightful King.

Exodus 6:1; 19:5, 6; 40:38; Psalm 136:11-14; Isaiah 42:1-4; 53:11, 12; Luke 1:32;
John 2:19; 10:11; 1 Corinthians 15:56, 57; 2 Corinthians 5:14; Philippians 2:7-11;
Colossians 1:24; Hebrews 2:9; 1 Peter 2:9, 10
Subject index: B.1, I.2, J.1
11 10 11 10 D
Suggested tune: *Danny Boy* aka *Londonderry Air*

97.   **Beyond the grief**

1   We pray for those among us who are grieving:
    feeling the force of sorrow's gnawing pain,
    finding no trace of hope or consolation
    beneath the weight of never-ending strain.

2   When every day is marred by empty aching –
    the unheard voice, the face no longer seen –
    Lord, may your Spirit's gentle touch bring closure
    for all that was and all that might have been.

3   As time goes on, give strength for readjustments:
    to face the truth when changes must be made.
    Through new perspectives, through supportive
      friendships,
    may signs of brighter futures be displayed.

4   Beyond the grief we ask for new tomorrows
    where bitter wounds are healed, and joy restored;
    where those we love, and we who mourn their passing,
    are safely cherished in your kindness, Lord.

Psalm 116:15; John 16:33; 2 Corinthians 1:3-5; 1 Thessalonians 4:13, 14
Subject index: F.5, H.3, J.2
11 10 11 10
Suggested tune: *O Perfect Love*

98. Light

1   We thank you, Christ our Lord,
for precious inward sight:
for grace and truth made known in you,
the true, eternal Light.

2   We ask the strength of heart
for what we know is right:
to take the daily discipline
of living in the light.

3   For wisdom, too, we pray,
till doubts are put to flight:
for complex and uncertain times
we need increasing light.

4   So keep our vision sharp,
however dark the night,
until we see you face to face
in pure, eternal light.

John 1:9, 17; 1 Corinthians 13:12; 2 Corinthians 4:6;
Philippians 3:16; James 1:5; 1 John 1:6, 7, 3:2
Subject index: B.1, H.6, F.5
6 6 8 6 (SM)
Suggested tune: *Carlisle*

99. **Inspire tomorrow's worship**

1   We who gather here are grateful
    for the richness of our past:
    thoughtful words, engaging music –
    we have loved them, held them fast.
    By your Spirit's steady nurture
    you have stirred your children's praise,
    prompting worship, faith and action
    through ten thousand yesterdays.

2   We who gather here are hopeful
    for the days that lie ahead:
    talents yet to be discovered,
    tunes unwritten, words unsaid.
    Grant the joys of fresh perspective;
    show what you would have us say
    to inspire tomorrow's worship,
    to enrich another day.

Psalms 33:1-3; 96:1; Ephesians 5:18-20; Colossians 3:16
Subject index: F.3, H.3
8 7 8 7 D
Suggested tune: *Bethany*

100. To see our neighbours

1   What are the stars to you, great God,
     but clouds of gas that flame and burn?
     They sparkle now in earth's dark night,
     yet each will surely fade in turn.

2   What is a mountain range to you
     but rocks heaped up against the sky?
     Will they not crumble down to dust,
     those crags so sharp, those peaks so high?

3   What of the trees, the flowers, the leaves
     whose beauty is your power displayed?
     You made them – yet their destiny
     consigns their splendour soon to fade.

4   What is the lion's roar to you?
     The eagle in its soaring flight?
     The untold marvels of the deep:
     are such as these your chief delight?

5   What is a human heart to you?
     A gem too precious to be lost!
     A jewel that you would die to own,
     to win, though so immense the cost!

6   Teach us to value all you made,
     to treat with care the things you prize –
     but most of all to share your love,
     to see our neighbours through your eyes.

Job 38–39; Psalm 8:1, 3, 4, 9; Matthew 13:44-46; 22:34;
Mark 10:45; Luke 10:36, 37; 2 Corinthians 5:14-16
Subject index: A.2, G.1, H.6
8 8 8 8 (LM)
Suggested tune: *Truro*

101. Unfinished drama

1 What can surpass this tale that our ears have heard?
God in a human life, as the living Word –
Jesus invites us, each one, to find our place
in his unfolding story of time and space.

2 Who can describe the sights that our eyes have seen?
Who can exhaust the richness of all they mean?
Symbol and sign show love in a hundred ways
as the truth is revealed to our searching gaze.

3 Here there are countless joys for the soul to find –
hope for the aching heart and the anxious mind;
glimpses and dreams of home that the future holds
as the unfinished drama of God unfolds.

4 Come, let your life enlarge his community –
multiple voices blending in unity,
partners in building all that the Lord intends
for the people he loves, that he calls his friends.

Jeremiah 29:13; Matthew 11:28-30; John 1:14; 14:1-3; 15:14, 15
Subject index: G.2, I.2, J.1
11 11 11 11
Suggested tune: *Water End* (adapted)

102. **Holy ground**

1   What holy ground! An upstairs room,
    a safe house in a hostile place:
    here Jesus brings his closest friends
    to share an evening face to face.

2   Watch as he kneels to wash their feet,
    with water and a towel at hand;
    hear as he warns of trials to come
    and threats they scarcely understand.

3   There he reshapes his people's past:
    see how he breaks and shares the bread;
    the wine becomes a sign of hope,
    beyond his pains, to joys ahead.

4   Then, look! He leads them from this room,
    for he must face life's darkest night,
    where raging powers of hell and state
    will try – and fail – to quench God's Light.

Matthew 26:17-35; Mark 14:12-31; Luke 22:7-23, 31-38; John 13:1-17; 15:18-25
Subject index: B.3, I.6
8 8 8 8 (M)
Suggested tune: *O Waly Waly*

103.   **A vital presence**

1   When Mary met the Lord on Easter morning
     she recognised him once he spoke her name:
     in spite of any change in his appearance,
     his kindness and his care were still the same;

2   and later, when he came to the disciples,
     no matter how securely locked the door,
     beyond their puzzlement and fear and doubting
     they recognised him by the wounds he bore;

3   and still he was their Teacher and Companion
     that morning on a Galilean beach
     when, over breakfast, he affirmed his friendship –
     transformed, and yet securely in their reach;

4   nor, after his ascension, did they hanker
     for times when they had seen him face to face:
     the coming of his promised Spirit brought them
     a vital presence nothing could displace;

5   and still he calls and leads his people onward,
     our wounded, risen Lord, our gracious Friend,
     his gentleness unchanged across the ages,
     his glory more than we can comprehend;

6   come, Lord! Remind us often of your closeness,
     and teach our hearts your truth, your life, your way,
     until, with joyful faith, we are accustomed
     to sense your holy presence day by day.

John 14:6; 20:14-16, 19-20; 21:1-14; Romans 5:5; Hebrews 13:5, 8
Subject index: B.6, H.6, I.1
11 10 11 10
Suggested tune: *Highwood*

104.   Until the storm

1   When pain or peril looms
     and dominates the day,
     where can I turn? Lord, show me then
     your wisdom and your way.

2   And when confusion blurs
     the plans I try to make,
     what shall I do? Let your word guide
     decisions I must take.

3   If panic starts to rise –
     the sentence of despair! –
     whom can I trust? You know my name;
     remind me of your care.

4   Should days ahead seem bleak
     and confidence be gone,
     how shall I cope? From you I ask
     the strength to carry on.

5   My fearful heart may scream,
     'This struggle is too rough –
     why this, why me?' You understand:
     and that must be enough.

6   So I will hide in you
     until the storm is spent –
     when will it pass? I know you know;
     in you I am content.

Psalms 55:2-5; 56:3, 10; 57:1; Isaiah 30:21; 43:1, 2; John 16:33; Hebrews 13:6
Subject index: F.5, G.3, H.3
6 6 8 6 (SM)
Suggested tune: *Franconia*

105.   Unfamiliar

1   When the unfamiliar beckons,
    stirring dreams of something new,
    Jesus, in each fresh adventure
    keep my focus fixed on you;
    as I leave the past behind me
    and the pains I should forget,
    help me yield to you my future;
    help me live without regret.

2   When the unfamiliar threatens
    and the pathway is unclear,
    when the darkness harbours danger,
    keep me mindful: you are near.
    Strengthened by your Spirit's presence
    and the wisdom you provide
    I will trust in you to guard me,
    I will trust in you to guide.

3   When the unfamiliar summons
    and it seems I have no choice,
    when the pressure feels unending,
    let me hear your calming voice.
    Lord of mystery, reassure me:
    you retain complete control,
    always calling me to follow,
    always nurturing my soul.

4   When the unfamiliar offers
    new demands, new ground to break,
    untried avenues of service,
    unexpected ways to take,
    let me then pursue obedience,
    learn to live as you intend,
    till life's final page is written,
    till I reach my journey's end.

Isaiah 43:1, 2, 18, 19; John 14:26; 16:33; Romans 8:28-30; 15:23;
Ephesians 5:10; Philippians 3:13, 14; Hebrews 12:2
Subject index: F.5, G.3, H.6
8 7 8 7 D
Suggested tune: *Rustington*

106.   Hiding place

1   When troubles bring distress,
    when landscapes shift and shake,
    I need a place to stand secure
    though mountains quake;
    when rising waters drive
    my search for higher ground,
    in you, as in some secret cave,
    my peace is found.

2   My bunker in the raid
    as warning sirens wail,
    my strongroom whose security
    can never fail,
    my safe house from the search
    when angry voices cry,
    on you, the God of endless strength,
    I can rely.

3   My shield from each assault,
    my haven from despair,
    my harbour from the raging seas,
    how well you care!
    My shelter from the storm,
    my shade from blazing sun,
    to you, the refuge of the weak,
    I gladly run.

4   The welcome of your smile,
    the kindness of your touch,
    reveal you as the faithful friend
    I need so much;
    the cover of your wings,
    the warmth of your embrace,
    assure me you will always be
    my hiding place.

Psalms 9:9; 18:2; 27:1, 5; 32:7; 46:1-3; 61:3, 4; 119:114; Isaiah 25:4
Subject index: F.5, G.3, H.2
6 6 8 4 D
Suggested tune: *Leoni*

107.   **Echoes of eternity**

1   When unexpected joy
     ignites the curious mind
     for new adventures, hopes and dreams
     the soul has yet to find,

2   or when untimely grief
     and unremitting pain
     expose our frail mortality
     and load the heart with strain,

3   then help us, Lord, to pause,
     to still our hearts, and hear
     the whisper that reminds the soul:
     eternity is near.

4   May we, creator God,
     begin to understand
     the timeless reach and cosmic breadth
     of all that you have planned,

5   till, humbled by your care,
     we learn to trust your grace,
     discerning in life's pains and joys
     our calling and our place;

6   till mystery leads to awe,
     and awe, to faith made strong
     through echoes of eternity
     and love's unfailing song.

Ecclesiastes 3:11; Hebrews 12:7; James 1:2, 3; 4:14; 1 Peter 1:6-9
Subject index: G.3, H.2, J.1
6 6 8 6 (SM)
Suggested tunes: *Sandys*; *St Thomas*

108. Fragrance

1   Where God's people live together
     sharing life with one accord,
     where their hearts desire the fragrance
     of the presence of their Lord,
     there he will bestow his blessing
     like anointing oil outpoured.

2   When God's people meet to praise him
     who knows what may happen there
     if some lavish act of worship
     spreads its fragrance everywhere,
     as when Mary, pouring perfume,
     wiped her Lord's feet with her hair?

3   When God's people go in mission,
     keen to make his message known,
     some will spurn the gospel's challenge,
     some will make his word their own,
     gathered to God's fragrant people
     round the Lord's eternal throne.

Psalm 133; John 12:3; 2 Corinthians 2:15
Subject index: F.5, H.6, I.1
8 7 8 7 8 7
Suggested tune: *Picardy*

109. Ransomed by the King

1 Who can join the soaring hymns that God has given us
  to sing?
 Who but those who are forgiven, who are ransomed by
  the King?
 Now released from debt and born again, how joyfully
  we bring
 our praises to the Lord:

  Sins forgiven, shackles broken,
  guilt removed and hearts restored;
  freely welcomed, heading homeward –
  thank you, Jesus, Saviour, Lord.

2 As we sing the songs of freedom, what a privilege we bear,
 one the brightest and the boldest of the angels cannot share!
 There is peace to drive our fear away, and hope for
  our despair
 in Jesus Christ our Lord:

3 He gives wisdom for our problems, he gives strength to
  face the fight;
 he is faithful, and he holds us though we stumble in
  the night;
 so with joyful, eager faith we wait to see the morning light,
 the coming of the Lord:

4 But the songs that God has given us are not for us alone:
 this is news for all the world, so let us make the gospel known
 till our neighbourhoods and nations bow in worship at
  the throne
 of Jesus Christ the Lord.

Psalm 103:1-4; Isaiah 35:4; Matthew 28:18, 19; John 8:32; 14:2, 3; Romans 5:1, 2;
Philippians 2:9-11, 16; 3:20; Colossians 1:13, 14; 1 Timothy 2:6; Titus 2:13;
Hebrews 2:16; 11:34; James 1:5; 2 Peter 3:12; Revelation 5:9, 10
Subject index: F.3, H.6, I.2
15 15 15 6 refrain 8 7 8 7
Suggested tune: *Battle Hymn of the Republic*

110.   Who dares

1   Who dares to stand where lightning arcs,
    where thunder booms and rolls,
    where skies ablaze with light and noise
    can daunt the staunchest souls?

2   Who dares to tread where tremors throb,
    where hill and headland shake,
    where mountains flame, where lava flows
    and landscapes bend and break?

3   Who dares approach the searing heat,
    the everlasting fire
    of God, the holy, living God,
    our Dread and our Desire?

4   Who dares to cross the searching beam
    and not recoil in fright
    before that dazzling, holy ray,
    God's penetrating sight?

5   Who dares resist the God who speaks,
    whose summons calls us near?
    God's welcome warms each open heart;
    God's love dispels our fear!

Exodus 19:16,18; Psalm 29:3-9; John 3:19, 20; Hebrews 12:18-22, 25, 29
Subject index: A.2, F.5
8 6 8 6 (CM)
Suggested tune: *Wiltshire*

111. Who is this

1   Who is this newborn child
here in a manger laid,
his birth announced by angel choirs
in splendid light arrayed?
    This is the mighty God,
    the Lord of time and space,
    who freely chooses to be born
    within the human race.

2   Who is this broken man
who wears a crown of thorn,
who walks the path to Calvary
accepting pain and scorn?
    This is the Lord of life
    whose triumph we declare,
    whose resurrection offers us
    eternal life to share.

3   Ascended now on high,
he reigns from heaven's throne,
for ultimate authority
belongs to him alone:
    his realm shall never end,
    his glory is assured,
    with every tongue acknowledging
    that Jesus Christ is Lord.

Matthew 27:29, 30; 28:18; Mark 15:17-19; Luke 1:32; 2:9-14; John 3:15, 16;
Acts 1:9; 1 Corinthians 15:20, 22, 25, 27; Philippians 2:11; Hebrews 1:3
Subject index: B.6, I.2
6 6 8 6 D (DSM)
Suggested tune: *St Mary* (Paul Leddington Wright)

112.   Fruitfully laden

1   Who makes a life bloom, showing God's goodness?
    Who causes joy and love to increase?
    Who but God's Spirit, planting and pruning,
    nurturing sweet and succulent peace?

2   Where there is love with patience and meekness,
    where we see joy with real self-control,
    there is the Spirit, tilling and tending,
    making God's children fruitful and whole.

3   Come, Holy Spirit, in and among us;
    sow the good seeds of kindness and care;
    bring us to harvest, fruitfully laden,
    filled with the love you call us to bear.

Galatians 5.22, 23
Subject index: C, F.5, H.1
10 9 10 9
Suggested tune: *Bunessan*

113. The mystery known as prayer

1 Why should we need to tell you
   our problems and our fears?
   You see beyond all distance,
   you live beyond all years;
      yet you are strangely willing
      to listen to our cares;
      you treat with solemn interest
      our rough, self-centred prayers.

2 How could we dare imagine
   that you should rearrange
   your plans for joy and justice
   when we think they should change?
      Yet tantalising glimpses
      of what you have in mind
      uncover dreams and visions
      to which we have been blind.

3 How can we ask for answers
   if wanting nothing more
   than slick and shallow comfort
   where life has left us sore?
      Yet, graciously, you show us
      the things we should have sought –
      not instant, easy blessings
      but asking as we ought.

4 You know the times we flounder
   with doubt or with dismay,
   when faith encounters struggle
   and shrinks in disarray.
      Lord, teach us by your Spirit,
      until we fully share
      the calling of your children,
      the mystery known as prayer.

Psalm 8:4; Isaiah 40:27, 28; 45:9-11; 57:15; Matthew 6:8; 9:24;
Luke 11:1; Romans 8:26, 27; James 4:3
Subject index:A.2, F.6, H.3
7 6 7 6 D
Suggested tune: *Salley Gardens*

114. Final Word

1 With eager minds and hearts we wait
  for all you want to say,
  amazed that still, Lord, you delight
  to speak to us today.

2 Inspire your preachers' careful words,
  enabling us to know
  the meaning of the holy text
  first written long ago.

3 Then may your Spirit probe and prompt
  with penetrating sight,
  to ground our listening to the truth
  in doing what is right.

4 So may our lives become a means
  by which your voice is heard,
  as living letters, sent by Christ,
  your full and final Word.

Psalms 119:18, 27, 60, 130, 166; 139:23, 24; Jeremiah 17:10; 29:13;
John 1:14; 13:17; 2 Corinthians 3:2, 3; 2 Timothy 2:12; Hebrews 1:1; 4:12
Subject index: A.4, E, I.2
8 6 8 6 (CM)
Suggested tune: *St Magnus*

115.   **All things new**

1   Within a fragile, hurting world
    where hunger, war and pain are rife,
    where hatred, greed and power conspire
    to undermine God's gift of life,
    and where those same destructive trends
    are lurking in our own hearts, too,
    how good to hear God's voice affirm
    the promise to make all things new.

2   How good to know that light has come –
    born here, the gracious Living Word:
    God's kindness shown in all he did;
    in all he said, God's welcome heard.
    By free surrender to a cross
    Christ saw his costly mission through;
    and now, in resurrection life,
    our Lord is making all things new.

3   The open invitation stands –
    hear how the call of Christ rings clear:
    to join God's great adventure now –
    the age to come is very near.
    So let this vision fire our hearts,
    reshape our thoughts, guide all we do:
    a word fulfilled, a world restored,
    the day when God makes all things new.

Jeremiah 17:9; Matthew 4:19; 24:6-8; Mark 1:15-17; John 1:1-5, 14; 6:37;
10:17, 18, 38; Romans 12:2; Revelation 1:18, 21:5
Subject index: A.3, G.2, J.3
8 8 8 8 D (DLM)
Suggested tune: *Jerusalem*

116.   Holy, faithful

1 You call us to be holy –
   available to you;
   you call us to be holy
   for you are holy, too.
        Lord, help us to be holy,
        our lives ablaze with grace,
        to bring your holy presence
        to this, our time, our place.

2 You call us to be faithful,
   to serve you every day;
   you call us to be faithful,
   obedient, come what may.
        Lord, help us to be faithful
        to all that we have heard
        from Christ, our master Teacher,
        your holy, faithful Word.

Leviticus 20:7; John 1:14; 13:13-17; 14:15;
2 Corinthians 2:14, 15; Philippians 1:21, 22
Subject index: A.3, H.6, I.2
7 6 7 6 D
Suggested tune: *Morning Light*

117.   You call us

1   You call us to be with you,
    to hear the words you say,
    allowing your instruction
    to shape us day by day.
        You summon our attention
        to watch the things you do,
        as in our daily living
        we learn to walk with you.

2   And as we get to know you,
    you challenge us to change,
    until your holy lifestyle
    no longer seems so strange.
        Within your gracious welcome
        we find, to our delight,
        the most unlikely people
        are precious in your sight.

3   How patiently you coax us
    beyond our doubt and fear,
    to model your compassion
    and make your message clear.
        You make so very fruitful
        the little we can give
        as your example shows us
        the way that we must live.

4   With bread and wine you promise
    forgiveness is assured –
    our love and our allegiance
    are yours forever, Lord!
        You draw us out to serve you
        wherever you may lead,
        believing you will guard us
        and meet our every need.

5   You promise to be with us,
     the risen Lord of all:
     you honour the obedience
     that does not shirk your call.
          We go with joy and purpose,
          your followers and friends,
          to give the world your offer
          of life that never ends.

Matthew 9:9-13; 10:1, 5-20; 26:26-28; 28:18-20; Mark 2:13-17; 3:14; 6:7-13;
14:22-24; Luke 6:30, 31; 9:1-6; 10:1-12; 17:10; 22:19, 20; John 20:21-23;
1 Corinthians 15:58; 2 Corinthians 5:18–6:2; 8:12
Subject index: B.3, H.6, I.6
7 6 7 6 D
Suggested tunes: *Thornbury*; *Aurelia*

118.   Sufficient courage

1   You came as one among us
unknown, unrecognised;
your teaching was disputed,
your way of life despised;
your neighbours and your family
had doubts that you were sane –
   give me sufficient courage
to share your lonely pain.

2   The guardians of tradition
disdained your steadfast choice
to give those at the margins
a value and a voice;
they scorned your proclamation
of broken lives made new –
   give me sufficient courage
to walk alongside you.

3   Then came the awful moment
the traitor showed his hand:
your friends succumbed to pressure
they could not understand.
In panic they abandoned
the call that drew them near –
   give me sufficient courage
to face the tests I fear.

4   The leaders of your people
insisted you must die,
and stifled thoughts of justice
with shouts of 'Crucify!'
The powers of state rejected
your claims, your words, your ways –
   give me sufficient courage
to serve you all my days.

Matthew 26:47-56; 27:22-26; Mark 3:21; 14:43-50; 15:9-15;
Luke 5:30; John 1:10, 11; 8:13
Subject index: B.3, G.3, H.4
7 6 7 6 D
Suggested tune: *Thornbury*

119. Faithful God

1 You, dear Lord, have made such kindness known,
   called us each by name to be your own;
   how clearly and how often you have shown,
   Father, you are a faithful God.

2 We have heard your voice, but turned away;
   still we hear you call, but still we stray;
   how firmly you remind us, day by day,
   to return to our faithful God.

3 Striving tirelessly, you win as friends
   rebels powerless to make amends –
   what love is this, a love which never ends?
   You are truly a faithful God!

4 Hear our grateful prayer, as we renew
   our resolve that we will trust in you,
   for we have found your gracious word rings true:
   Father, you are a faithful God.

Psalm 95:8-10; Hosea 14:1; Romans 5:8-10; 1 Corinthians 1:9;
2 Corinthians 5:14, 19; Titus 1:2; 3:4; Hebrews 3:8-10; 1 John 3:1
Subject index: A.5, F.4, G.2
9 9 10 8
Suggested tune: *Salut d'Amour*

120.   We thank you, Lord

1   You gave us life itself
    and all we need to live –
    yet rarely do we recognise
    how eagerly you give.

2   When shelter, food and health
    are all we really need,
    we thank you, Lord: your daily gifts
    are generous indeed.

3   On life's uncertain paths,
    in every complex choice,
    we thank you, Lord, for times we hear
    your patient, guiding voice.

4   The crises we must face,
    the heartaches we endure –
    we thank you, Lord, that come what may
    in you we stand secure.

5   The guilt we cannot hide,
    the flaws we fail to see –
    we thank you, Lord, that you forgive;
    your mercy makes us free.

6   Now may our hearts be stirred,
    our vision be renewed,
    remembering our debt to you
    in daily gratitude.

Psalms 32:1; 103:1-5; Isaiah 30:21; John 16:33; Acts 17:25;
Romans 8:28; 1 Timothy 6:17; James 1:5
Subject index: F.4, G.1, H.3
6 6 8 6 (SM)
Suggested tunes: *Sandys; St Thomas*

121. Come what may

1 You give us times of joy
and cause for celebration
when life's unfolding scenes
give moments of elation.
    When we are prospering
    and peace adorns our days,
    may our contentment bloom
    in songs of thankful praise.

2 But sometimes we are stalked
by unremitting sorrow,
as trouble, fear or grief
cast shadows on tomorrow –
    beneath the weight of stress
    we never chose to bear,
    we search for shards of hope,
    reminders of your care.

3 When times of bliss are tinged
with unexpected aching,
or when, through bleakest gloom,
the dawn of hope is breaking,
    help us to grasp afresh
    how you turn bad to good
    till, on life's changing tides,
    we trust you as we should.

4 When we recall our past,
your faithfulness astounds us!
And now, and till life's end,
your watchful love surrounds us.
    However dark the night,
    however bright the day,
    Lord Jesus, give us faith
    to trust you, come what may.

Genesis 50:20; Deuteronomy 8:10-11; Psalm 16:6; Habakkuk 3:16, 17;
John 16:33; Romans 8:38, 39; Hebrews 12:7; James 1:2-4; 1 Peter 1:6, 7; 5:7
Subject index: F.4, G.3, H.4
6 7 6 7 6 6 6 6
Suggested tunes: *Nun Danket*; *Gracias*

122. Fresh beginnings

1 You, Lord, speak of fresh beginnings,
  hope rekindled, joy made new,
  ancient wonders overshadowed
  as you prove your promise true.

2 You, Lord, speak of barren deserts
  brought to life as rivers flow;
  and for pilgrims in the wasteland
  you provide the way to go.

3 You, Lord, speak of precious children,
  chosen, rescued, homeward bound,
  from whose hearts – refreshed, excited –
  songs of praise and thanks resound.

4 You, Lord, speak of fresh beginnings,
  fruitful deserts, lives restored;
  answering your gracious summons,
  we will follow you, our Lord.

Isaiah 43:18-21
Subject index: A.5, F.5, H.1
8 7 8 7
Suggested tune: *Stuttgart*

123. The powers that daunt

1 You only can discern the powers
 that daunt the troubled soul –
 Lord, by your Spirit speak the words
 that make the wounded whole.

2 When lives are blighted by the scars
 of wrongs done long ago,
 Lord, may your Spirit's comfort bring
 the peace we yearn to know.

3 When half-formed dread with no clear root
 engenders deep unease,
 Lord, grant your Spirit's kiss of peace
 to quell such moods as these.

4 In neighbourhoods ensnared by fear,
 where evil forces roam,
 Lord, set your Spirit's calming touch
 on every heart and home.

5 And where our very land seems stained
 from blood unjustly shed,
 Lord, by your Spirit heal and cleanse –
 grant joy and growth instead.

6 You only can discern the force
 of these unsettling powers –
 Lord, may your Spirit change our hearts
 until your peace is ours.

Deuteronomy 21:1-9; 1 Samuel 32:18; Isaiah 61:1-4; John 16:33
Subject index: G.2, H.3, J.1
8 6 8 6 (CM)
Suggested tune: *St Fulbert*

124. Yearnings

1 You recognise my hopes and dreams,
      a human heart's desire;
   you see the yearnings, good and bad,
      that set my soul on fire;

2 with gentle, holy scrutiny
      you probe my inmost heart;
   my best defences, stormed by love,
      so swiftly fall apart;

3 then in the seed-bed of my life
      I find new yearnings sown
   as, nurtured by your Spirit's care,
      the life of heaven is grown;

4 till you, Lord, are my one desire –
      one you alone can meet;
   redeemed, refocused and renewed,
      in you I stand complete.

Psalms 103:3-5; 139:3, 4; Proverbs 20:27; Jeremiah 17:9, 10;
Matthew 13:23; Mark 4:20; Luke 8:15; James 1:21
Subject index: F.5, G.2, H.1
8 6 8 6 (CM)
Suggested tunes: *St Agnes* (Dykes); *Westminster* (Turle)

125.   **Yours is the kingdom**

1   Yours is the kingdom: not a realm of this age,
    built on a broken world's prowess or fame,
    nor made secure by treaties, wars or taxes –
    you hold the kingdom in your Father's name.

2   Yours is the power that dwarfs the strongest armies,
    mightier than any earthly sword or shield,
    mightier by far than politics or riches:
    it is the power of suffering love you wield.

3   Yours is the glory: not in this world's honours –
    glory of love embracing utter loss,
    glory whose depth defies imagination:
    the glory seen, Lord Jesus, at your cross.

Matthew 6:13; John 5:22, 23; 12:23, 24; 17:1; 18:36
Subject index: B.3, F.2, J.1
11 10 11 10
Suggested tunes: *Highwood; O Perfect Love*

Appendix and Indexes

Appendix: Sources of Suggested Tunes

The following list is not exhaustive, but is designed to indicate one or more books in which the named tunes can be found. Many of these tunes will also be found in numerous other standard hymnals; and in the case of some of the hymnals in this list, many standard tunes will be found but are not listed here. For unpublished suggested tunes, contact the author via Kevin Mayhew Ltd.

Abbots Leigh	AMRW, CH4, HOAN, P, R&S, STF	Fulda	AMRW, CH4, HOAN, P, R&S, STF
		Gatescarth	R&S, STF
Aberystwyth	AMRW, CH4, HOAN, P, R&S, STF	Go Forth	H&P, HTC
		Gonfalon Royal	AMRW, CH4, HOAN, P, R&S, STF
Abingdon	HOAN, R&S, STF		
All for Jesus	AMRW, CH4, HOAN, P, R&S, STF	Gott ein Vater (Pastor Pastorum)	AMRW, HOAN
		Gott Will's Machen	AMRW, CH4, HOAN, STF
All Saints	AMRW, P, R&S, STF	Gower Street Chapel	P
Angel Voices	AMRW, CH4, HOAN, P, R&S, STF	Gracias	AMRW, HOAN, STF
		Greensleeves	AMRW, HOAN, P, R&S
Aurelia	AMRW, CH4, HOAN, P, R&S, STF	Highwood	AMRW, CH4, P, R&S, STF
Battle Hymn of the Republic	AMRW, CH4, HOAN, P	Hyfrydol	AMRW, CH4, HOAN, P, R&S, STF
		Intercessor	AMRW, CH4, P, R&S
Bethany	HOAN, P, R&S, STF	Irish	AMRW, CH4, HOAN, P, R&S, STF
Blaenwern	AMRW, CH4, HOAN, P, R&S, STF	Jerusalem	AMRW, CH4, HOAN, P, STF
Bunessan	AMRW, CH4, HOAN, P, R&S, STF	Kelvingrove	AMRW, CH4, HOAN, P, R&S, STF
Carlisle	AMRW, CH4, HOAN, P, R&S, STF	Kingsfold	AMRW, CH4, HOAN, P, R&S, STF
Chilton Foliat	CH4, R&S	Leoni	AMRW, CH4, HOAN, P, R&S, STF
Christe Sanctorum	AMRW, CH4, HOAN, P, R&S, STF	Little Cornard	AMRW, CH4, HOAN, P, STF
		Lobe den Herren	AMRW, CH4, HOAN, P, R&S, STF
Church Triumphant	AMRW, CH4, HOAN, P, R&S		
		Love Divine	AMRW, HOAN, P, R&S
Coe Fen	AMRW, CH4, HOAN, P, R&S, STF	Luckington	AMRW, CH4, HOAN, P, R&S, STF
Corvedale	AMRW, STF	Melcombe	AMRW, CH4, HOAN, P, R&S, STF
Danny Boy (Londonderry Air)	AMRW, CH4, HOAN, P, R&S, STF	Melita	AMRW, CH4, HOAN, P, R&S, STF
		Morning Light	AMRW, HOAN, P, STF
Duke Street	AMRW, CH4, HOAN, P, R&S, STF	Nun Danket	AMRW, CH4, HOAN, P, R&S, STF
Earth and All Stars	AMRW, CH4	O Perfect Love	AMRW, HOAN, P, STF
Ellacombe	AMRW, CH4, HOAN, STF	O Waly Waly	AMRW, CH4, HOAN, STF
Engleberg	AMRW, CH4, R&S, STF	Patrixbourne	AMRW, HTC
Ephraim	H&P, NRH, P	Picardy	AMRW, CH4, HOAN, R&S, STF
Epiphany Hymn (Epiphany)	AMRW, CH4, HOAN, P, R&S, STF	Repton	AMRW, CH4, HOAN, R&S, STF
		Rustington	AMRW, HOAN, P, R&S, STF
Finlandia	AMRW, CH4, HOAN, P, STF	Salley Gardens	AMRW, CH4
Franconia	AMRW, HOAN, P, R&S, STF	Salut d'Amour	SSC

Sandys	AMRW, CH4, HOAN, R&S, STF	Trentham	HOAN, P, STF
Shipston	AMRW, CH4, HOAN, R&S, STF	Truro	AMRW, CH4, HOAN, P, R&S, STF
Slane	AMRW, CH4, HOAN, P, R&S, STF	University	AMRW, HOAN, P, R&S, STF
Spiritus Vitae	AMRW, HOAN, P, R&S, STF	Vision	CH4, STF
St Agnes *(Dykes)*	AMRW, CH4, HOAN, P	Vox Dilecti	CH4, HOAN, P, STF
St Bernard	AMRW, HOAN, P, R&S, STF	Vreuchten	AMRW, CH4, P, R&S, STF
St Denio	AMRW, CH4, HOAN, P, R&S, STF	Water End	SP
St Fulbert	AMRW, CH4, HOAN, P, R&S, STF	West Ashton	AMRW, NS
St Leonard's *(Gould)*	AMRW, HOAN, P, STF	Westminster *(Turle)*	AMRW, HOAN, R&S
St Magnus	AMRW, CH4, HOAN, P, R&S, STF	Wiltshire	AMRW, CH4, HOAN, P, R&S, STF
St Mary *(Paul Leddington Wright)*	STF	Winchester New	AMRW, CH4, HOAN, P, R&S, STF
St Peter	AMRW, CH4, HOAN, R&S, STF	Wolvercote	AMRW, CH4, HOAN, P, R&S, STF
St Thomas	AMRW, P, R&S	Woodlands	AMRW, CH4, HOAN, P, R&S, STF
Stowey	CH4, HOAN, P, R&S, STF	Worthy the Lamb	NRH, SHF
Stuttgart	AMRW, CH4, HOAN, P, STF	Yorkshire (Stockport)	AMRW, HOAN, P, R&S, STF
Sussex	AMRW, HOAN, R&S, STF		
Thaxted	AMRW, CH4, HOAN, P, STF	Zimbabwe *(John Bell)*	HOAN
Thornbury	AMRW, CH4, HOAN, P, R&S, STF		
Thorpe	SGP1		

Key

AMRW	Ancient & Modern: Hymns & Songs for Refreshing Worship (Hymns Ancient & Modern Ltd, 2013)
CH4	Church Hymnary, 4th Edition (Canterbury Press, 2005)
H&P	Hymns & Psalms (Methodist Publishing House, 1983)
HOAN	Hymns Old and New: One Church, One Faith, One Lord (Kevin Mayhew, 2004)
HTC	Hymns for Today's Church: 2nd Edition (Jubilate Hymns/Hodder & Stoughton, 1987)
NRH	New Redemption Hymnal (Word (UK), 1986)
NS	New Start Hymns and Songs (Kevin Mayhew, 1999)
P	Praise! (Praise Trust, 2000)
R&S	Rejoice & Sing (United Reformed Church/Oxford University Press, 1991)
SGP1	Songs of God's People, Volume 1 (Kevin Mayhew, 2001)
SHF	Songs & Hymns of Fellowship (Thankyou Music/Kingsway Music, 1987)
SP	Songs of Praise – Enlarged Edition (Oxford University Press, 1931)
SSC	Songs for a Servant Church (Kevin Mayhew, 2015)
STF	Singing the Faith (Hymns Ancient & Modern Ltd for Trustees for Methodist Church Purposes, 2011)

Metrical Index

Metre	Tune(s)	First line	No
5 5 5 4 D	Bunessan	Jesus our Teacher	48
6 5 6 5	Gott ein Vater	Sprinkle me with water	78
6 6 6 6 8 8	Little Cornard	Here is another day	36
	Little Cornard	Teach us to know your heart	79
6 6 6 6 refrain 8 8	Little Cornard	Lord of the word of life	61
6 6 8 4 D	Leoni	When troubles bring distress	106
6 6 8 6 (SM)	Trentham	How dark it is, this night	41
	Sandys	In times of stress and grief	46
	Sandys	Lord Jesus, Teacher, speak	60
	St Thomas	The summer cools and fades	90
	Carlisle	We thank you, Christ our Lord	98
	Franconia	When pain or peril looms	104
	Sandys; St Thomas	When unexpected joy	107
	Sandys; St Thomas	You gave us life itself	120
6 6 8 6 D (DSM)	St Mary (Paul Leddington Wright)	Who is this newborn child	111
6 7 6 7 6 6 6 6	Nun Danket; Gracias	You give us times of joy	121
6 7 6 7 D	Vreuchten	Lord Jesus, Living Word	59
7 6 7 6 7 7 7 6	Kelvingrove	Lord, forgive! We have not grasped	56
7 6 7 6 D	Thornbury	Did you not send your Spirit	12
	Wolvercote	Does love have more to offer	14
	Aurelia	From empty shells of worship	21
	Salley Gardens	I offered you an acorn	44
	Salley Gardens	The flow of time is pulsing	86
	Ellacombe	To Abram came a promise	92
	Salley Gardens	Why should we need to tell you	113
	Morning Light	You call us to be holy	116
	Thornbury; Aurelia	You call us to be with you	117
	Thornbury	You came as one among us	118
7 6 7 6 Triple	Thaxted	A man walked through a garden	1
	Thaxted	The peace of God be with you	89
7 7 7 6 D		Be gracious to us, Father	5
7 7 7 7	Ephraim	Light a candle, tend its flame	50
7 7 7 7 D	Aberystwyth	Jesus, true and living bread	49
7 7 8 7		To Jerusalem he rides	93
8 4 8 4 8 8 8 4	Worthy the Lamb	God whose open-handed giving	29
8 5 8 5 8 7	Angel Voices	God whose ways surpass the visions	30
	Angel Voices	Holy Father, may your presence	38
8 6 8 4 4 6 8 6		Lord Christ, you honoured human flesh	52
8 6 8 6 (CM)	University	For times when we have work to do	20
	St Peter	Pause here a while and contemplate	73
	Irish	The call of Christ is death and life	83
	St Bernard	The One we follow gladly chose	88
	Wiltshire	Who dares to stand where lightning arcs	110
	St Magnus	With eager minds and hearts we wait	114
	St Fulbert	You only can discern the powers	123

Metre	Tune(s)	First line	No
	St Agnes (Dykes); Westminster (Turle)	You recognise my hopes and dreams	124
8 6 8 6 6 6 8 6	*Zimbabwe (John Bell)*	Lord, every day may we discern	54
8 6 8 6 D (DCM)	*Mornington Crescent (Oliver Tarney); Kingsfold*	A preacher came from Nazareth	2
	Coe Fen	God, grant to us a sense of place	25
	Coe Fen	How stubbornly the human heart	42
	Kingsfold	The beauty of your holiness	82
	Vox Dilecti	The journey is too far for us	87
8 6 8 8 6	*Gatescarth*	Father, by your commanding voice	18
	Gatescarth	Lord, you've invited us to come	62
	Repton	The ancient prophets searched for Christ	81
8 7 8 5	*St Leonard's (Gould)*	From the wealth of your provision	23
	St Leonard's (Gould)	In the stillness of the morning	45
8 7 8 7	*Sussex*	Broken tunes from trembling voices	8
	All for Jesus	Flowing water, flowing water	19
	Shipston	From the garden to the city	22
	Gott Will's Machen	God beyond us: who can fathom	24
	All for Jesus	God of mercy, show us kindness	26
	Love Divine	Holy, holy, holy Father	39
	Stuttgart	You, Lord, speak of fresh beginnings	122
8 7 8 7 7 7	*Patrixbourne; All Saints*	God who freed a captive people	28
8 7 8 7 8 7	*Picardy*	Where God's people live together	108
8 7 8 7 D	*Corvedale; Bethany*	Dare you follow if he leads you	10
	Hyfrydol; Blaenwern	Drenched in light, a rustic manger	16
	Unnamed tune by Paul Drinkwater; Abbots Leigh	Someone told me of a Saviour	77
	Bethany	We who gather here are grateful	99
	Rustington	When the unfamiliar beckons	105
8 8 8 6 6 7 10 7 8	*Greensleeves*	God's gift to us today is love	32
8 8 8 7 8 7		The call of Jesus Christ rings clear	84
8 8 8 8 (LM)	*Melcombe; Fulda*	Ahead we see an open door	3
	Fulda	Come, taste the wine of lasting joy	9
	Gonfalon Royal; Winchester New	Disturb us, Lord, from easy lives	13
	Gonfalon Royal	Lord Christ, you walked our dusty streets	53
	Church Triumphant	My God, within your love I find	66
	O Waly Waly	Once I was far, so far from you	69
	Duke Street	Our ears have heard the voice of hope	71
	Melcombe	Proclaim the death of Christ the Lord	74
	Truro	What are the stars to you, great God	100
	O Waly Waly	What holy ground! An upstairs room	102
8 8 8 8 5	*Flaunden (John Barnard)*	Beyond the faintest distant star	6
8 8 8 8 8 8	*New Kendal (Mike Haines); Melita*	Help us, Lord Jesus, here to weld	35
	Abingdon	My Lord, I bring my all to you	67
	Melita	No power can drain the Christian's joy	68
8 8 8 8 D (DLM)	*Jerusalem*	Within a fragile, hurting world	115
9 8 9 8	*Spiritus Vitae*	God, outside time yet always present	27
	Spiritus Vitae	Unveil again your holy mystery	95
9 9 10 8	*Salut d'Amour*	You, dear Lord, have made such kindness known	119

Scriptural Index

Ref	Page
22:34	100
22:37	52, 84
24:6-8	58, 115
25:31-40	40
25:34-36	87
25:40	4
26:6-13	4
26:17-21	4
26:17-35	102
26:20-29	49, 95
26:26-28	23, 117
26:26-29	3
26:36-39	1
26:36-46	41
26:36-47	95
26:36-56	10
26:39	63
26:45, 46	59
26:47-56	118
26:55, 56	95
26:58	10
26:69-75	10
27:22-26	118
27:29, 30	111
27:30	93
28:1	10
28:17, 18	91
28:18	111
28:18, 19	109
28:18-20	58, 117
28:19	71
28:19, 20	48
28:20	83

Mark

Ref	Page
1:14	63
1:15	2
1:15-17	115
1:40-42	53
2:13-17	117
2:14	16
2:27	86
3:5	2
3:14	117
3:21	118
4:19	13
4:20	124
4:33	24
4:40	54
6:7-13	117
6:30-43	24
6:32-37	87
8:31	2, 93
8:34	70
8:34, 35	2, 83
9:2-8	16
9:31	73
9:41	4
10:32-34	93
10:42	55
10:43, 44	20, 65
10:45	81, 88, 100
11:1-10	4
11:7-10	93
12:17	84
12:29-30	52
12:30	67
12:30, 31	84
14:3-9	4
14:12-18	4
14:12-25	3
14:12-31	102
14:17-25	95
14:18-25	49
14:22-24	23, 117
14:32-36	1
14:32-42	41
14:32-44	95
14:32-50	10
14:36	63
14:41-42	59
14:43-50	118
14:49, 50	95
14:54	10
14:66-72	10
15:9-15	118
15:17-19	111
15:24	93
15:37	93
16:1, 2	10
16:3, 4	91
16:15	71
16:15, 16	58

Luke

Ref	Page
1:1-4	81
1:32	96, 111
1:35	92
1:78, 79	49
2:5-7	92
2:7-16	16
2:9-14	111
2:51, 52	63
5:12, 13	53
5:27	16
5:30	118
6:30, 31	117
6:38	44
6:43-45	62
8:9	18
8:14	13
8:15	124
9:1-6	117
9:2	2
9:12-17	24
9:22	73, 93
9:23	70
9:23, 24	83
9:28-35	16
9:44	73
10:1	2
10:1-12	117
10:9	2
10:36, 37	40, 100
11:1	113
11:2	56
11:3	23
12:6, 7	9
12:8, 9	83
12:15	57
12:28-31	54
12:29-31	23
12:32	63
14:33	91
17:5	35
17:10	84, 117
18:9-14	21
18:31-33	93
19:10	81
19:28-36	4
19:35-38	93
20:25	84
22:7-15	4
22:7-23	102
22:14-20	3
22:15-23	95
22:19, 20	23, 117
22:19-21	49
22:31-38	102
22:39-44	1
22:39-46	10, 41
22:39-48	95
22:42	63
22:54-62	10
23:33	93, 95
23:46	93
24:1, 2	10
24:1-3	91
24:11, 12	10
24:13-16	91
24:19	93
24:26	93
24:28-32	91
24:34	10
24:44	74
24:47	75

John

Ref	Page
1:1	61
1:1-3	7
1:1-5	115
1:4	92
1:9	50, 98
1:10, 11	118
1:10-12	59
1:11	63
1:14	16, 18, 24, 37, 52, 61, 63, 81, 92, 101, 114, 115, 116
1:17	98
1:18	16
1:43	16
1:45	2
2:1-11	37

4:7	84	6:10	35	4:5-9	89
4:10	88	6:14	52	4:7	66
11:1	20, 52, 77				

Ephesians

Colossians

11:23-25	87	1:4, 5	66	1:13	19, 52, 69
11:23-26	49, 74, 95	1:13, 14	7	1:13, 14	43, 109
11:26	15	1:18, 19	27	1:14	70
12:7	84	1:19, 20	53	1:15-17	7
12:13	12	2:8, 9	82	1:17	6
13:7	32	2:13	69	1:23	54
13:12	38, 98	2:14	49	1:24	96
14:15	35	2:14-18	22	1:27	49
15:3, 4	74	2:15-17	71	2:7	62
15:20	68, 93, 111	3:4, 5	27	2:15	51
15:20-23	90	3:17-19	32	3:16	99
15:22	52, 111	3:19	94	3:17	20, 36, 78
15:24-26	93	4:1	70	3:23	20, 56
15:25	51, 111	4:3, 4	25		
15:26	52	4:3-5	12		
15:27	111	4:18, 19	55		

1 Thessalonians

15:56, 57	96	4:24	44	4:13, 14	97
15:58	51, 117	4:31	76	4:17	43
		5:1	12, 80		

2 Corinthians

1 Timothy

		5:2	14		
1:3-5	97	5:8-12	87	1:16	66
1:20	74	5:10	27, 36, 60, 65, 79,	2:1	35
2:14, 15	116		80, 85, 105	2:6	109
2:15	108	5:15, 16	25	4:7	21
3:2, 3	114	5:18-20	99	6:7	57
3:18	39	6:12	87	6:16	64
4:6	50, 98	6:13	15	6:17	57, 75, 120

Philippians

2 Timothy

4:7-10	68				
4:13	54	1:6	42	2:11, 12	26
4:17, 18	70	1:9, 10	27	2:11-13	83
5:7	87	1:9-11	11	2:12	114
5:10	38	1:21	2, 48	2:15	61
5:14	96, 119	1:21, 22	116	3:7	21
5:14, 15	94	2:3	13, 25, 53	3:16, 17	61
5:14-16	100	2:5-7	65	4:7	2
5:17	26, 71	2:6, 7	14		

Titus

5:17, 18	66	2:7	20		
5:18-21	117	2:7-11	96	1:2	54, 119
5:19	22, 70, 119	2:8-11	51	2:13	109
5:20	56	2:9-11	109	2:14	80
6:1, 2	117	2:10-11	2	3:4	119
8:12	117	2:11	111		
10:5	65	2:12	56		
13:4	68	2:13	9, 39		

Hebrews

Galatians

		2:15	50	1:1	61, 114
2:16	71	2:16	109	1:1, 2	18
2:20	51, 77	3:7, 8	70	1:3	37, 111
4:4	81, 92	3:7-9	66	1:8, 9	22
4:4, 5	73	3:8-11	54	1:9	49
4:9	57	3:12-14	22	2:8, 9	74
4:19	44	3:13-14	70, 80, 105	2:9	51, 96
5:1	71	3:16	33, 98	2:10, 11	52
5:16-18	7	3:19	21	2:14, 15	43
5:22-23	112	3:20	22, 70, 109	2:14-18	49
6:2	25, 40, 50			2:16	109
6:5	50			2:17	90
6:9, 10	36				

Church Year Index

Trinity

Harvest

Remembrance

Subject Index

Thematic Index

Index of First Lines and Titles

First lines are in ordinary type; titles in italics and indented.
Titles are not included where they match the opening of the first line.